ANNOUNCING THE HAVERGAL EDITION
NOW IN PREPARATION FOR PUBLICATION

The edition of *The Complete Works of Frances Ridley Havergal* has five parts:

Volume I *Behold Your King:*
              The Complete Poetical Works of Frances Ridley Havergal

Volume II *Whose I Am and Whom I Serve:*
              Prose Works of Frances Ridley Havergal

Volume III *Loving Messages for the Little Ones:*
              Works for Children by Frances Ridley Havergal

Volume IV *Love for Love: Frances Ridley Havergal:*
              Memorials, Letters and Biographical Works

Volume V *Songs of Truth and Love:*
              Music by Frances Ridley Havergal and William Henry Havergal

David L. Chalkley, Editor   Dr. Glen T. Wegge, Music Editor

The Music of Frances Ridley Havergal by Glen T. Wegge, Ph.D.

This Companion Volume to the Havergal edition is a valuable presentation of F.R.H.'s extant scores. Except for a very few of her hymntunes published in hymnbooks, most or nearly all of F.R.H.'s scores have been very little—if any at all—seen, or even known of, for nearly a century. What a valuable body of music has been unknown for so long and is now made available to many. Dr. Wegge completed his Ph.D. in Music Theory at Indiana University at Bloomington, and his diligence and thoroughness in this volume are obvious. First an analysis of F.R.H.'s compositions is given, an essay that both addresses the most advanced musicians and also reaches those who are untrained in music; then all the extant scores that have been found are newly typeset, with complete texts for each score and extensive indices at the end of the book. This volume presents F.R.H.'s music in newly typeset scores diligently prepared by Dr. Wegge, and Volume V of the Havergal edition presents the scores in facsimile, the original 19th century scores. (The essay—a dissertation—analysing her scores is given the same both in this Companion Volume and in Volume V of the Havergal edition.) m

    Dr. Wegge is also preparing all of these scores for publication in performance folio editions.

not heard shall they consider.

CHAPTER LIII.

WHO hath believed our report? and to whom is the arm of the LORD revealed? 2 For he shall grow up before him as a tender plant, and as a root out of a dry ground: he hath no form nor comeliness; and when we shall see him, there is no beauty that we should desire him. 3 He is despised and rejected of men; a man of sorrows, and acquainted with grief: and we hid as it were our faces from him; he was despised, and we esteemed him not. 4 Surely he hath borne our griefs, and carried our sorrows: yet we did esteem him stricken, smitten of God, and afflicted. 5 But he was wounded for our transgressions, he was bruised for our iniquities: the chastisement of our peace was upon him; and with his stripes we are healed. 6 All we, like sheep, have gone astray; we have turned every one to his own way; and the LORD hath laid on him the iniquity of us all. 7 He was oppressed, and he was afflicted, yet he opened not his mouth: he is brought as a lamb to the slaughter, and as a sheep before her shearers is dumb, so he openeth not his mouth.

8 He was taken from prison and from judgment: and who shall declare his generation? for he was cut off out of the land of the living: for the trans-

the LORD of hosts is his name; and thy Redeemer the Holy One of Israel; The God of the whole earth shall he be called. 6 For the LORD hath called thee as a woman forsaken and grieved in spirit, and a wife of youth, when thou wast refused, saith thy God. 7 For a small moment have I forsaken thee; but with great mercies will I gather thee. 8 In a little wrath I hid my face from thee for a moment; but with everlasting kindness will I have mercy on thee, saith the LORD thy Redeemer. 9 For this is as the waters of Noah unto me: for as I have sworn that the waters of Noah should no more go over the earth; so have I sworn that I would not be wroth with thee, nor rebuke thee. 10 For the mountains shall depart, and the hills be removed; but my kindness shall not depart from thee, neither shall the covenant of my peace be removed, saith the LORD that hath mercy on thee. 11 O thou afflicted, tossed with tempest, and not comforted, behold, I will lay thy stones with fair colours, and lay thy foundations with sapphires. 12 And I will make thy windows of agates, and thy gates of carbuncles, and all thy borders of pleasant stones. 13 And all thy children shall be taught of the LORD; and great shall be the peace of thy children. 14 In righteousness shalt thou be estab-

y 2 Co. 4. 17.
z Lu. 23. 18, &c.
a He. 4. 15.
κ as a hiding of faces from him, or, from us;
λ or, he hid his face from us.
b Mat. 26. 37.
θ or, tormented.
c Ro. 11. 29.
μ bruise.
d 1 Pe. 2. 24, 25.
e 2 Sa. 23. 5.
ν made the iniquities of us all to meet on him.
f Ro. 4. 25.
g 1 Pe. 3. 18.
h Re. 21. 18.
θ Ac. 8. 32. 35.
π or, away by distress and judgment: but who.
i John 6. 45.
k Da. 9. 26.

Part of the page that has Isaiah 53 and 54 in F.R.H.'s last Bagster study Bible.

"One Hour with Jesus" and Encouragements to Bible Study

BY

Frances Ridley Havergal,

AND

Mrs. Stephen Menzies,

AND

Robert Murray M'Cheyne

"One Hour with Jesus" by Frances Ridley Havergal

Hints on Bible Marking by Mrs. Stephen Menzies

My Bible Study: for the Sundays of the Year by F.R.H.

"The Means of Growth" by F.R.H.

Robert Murray M'Cheyne's Bible Reading Calendar

CONTENTS.

"Knowing her intense desire that Christ should be magnified, whether
by her life or in her death, may it be to His glory
that in these pages she, being dead,
'Yet speaketh !' "

Taken from the Edition of *The Complete Works of Frances Ridley Havergal.*

David L. Chalkley, Editor   Dr. Glen T. Wegge, Associate Editor

ISBN 978-1-937236-05-2   Library of Congress: 2011939756

Book cover by Sherry Goodwin and David Carter.

Note: This book has suggestions to help, but never requirements nor
legalistic yokes. Please read M'Cheyne's fourth point on page 65.

ONE HOUR WITH JESUS.

"What! could ye not watch with Me one hour?"

BY

FRANCES RIDLEY HAVERGAL.

LONDON:

S. W. PARTRIDGE & CO. PATERNOSTER ROW.

NISBET & CO., 21, BERNERS STREET.

BIRMINGHAM: C. CASWELL.

ONE PENNY.

The First Epistle general of JOHN.

A.D. 90.

CHAPTER I.

THAT which was from the *a* beginning, which we *b* have heard, which we have seen *c* with our eyes, which we have looked upon, and our hands have *d* handled, of the Word of life;

2 (For the life was manifested, and we have seen it, and bear witness, and shew unto you that eternal life,*f* which was with the Father, and was manifested unto us;)

3 That which we have seen and heard declare we unto you, that ye also may have fellowship with us: and truly our fellowship *i* is with the Father, and with his Son Jesus Christ.

4 And these things write we unto you, that *i* your joy may be full.

5 This then is the message which we have heard of him, and declare unto you, that God is light,*r* and in him is no darkness at all.

6 If we say that we have fellowship with him, and walk in darkness, we lie, and do not the truth: *Jo. 9. 12. 9.* *12. 4. 5.*

7 But if we walk *i* in the light, as he is in the light, we have fellowship one with another, and the blood *x* of Jesus Christ his Son cleanseth us from all sin. *He. 12. 12.*

8 If we say that we have no sin,*y* we deceive ourselves, and the truth is not in us.

9 If we confess *z* our sins, he is faithful and just *i* to forgive us our sins, and to cleanse *i* us from all unrighteousness. *Is. 6. 7.*

10 If we say that we have not sinned, we make him a liar, and his word is not in us.

CHAPTER II.

MY little children, these things write I unto you, that ye sin not. And if any man sin,*i* we have an advocate*f* with the Father, Jesus Christ the righteous:*g* *2. 3. 89.*

2 And he is the propitiation*g* for our sins; and not for our's only, but also for the sins of the whole world.

3 And hereby we do know that we know him, if we keep *k* his commandments.

4 He that saith, I know him, and keepeth not his commandments, is a liar, and the truth is not in him.

5 But whoso keepeth his word, in him verily is the love of God perfected: hereby know we that we are in him.

6 He that saith he abideth *m* in him, ought himself also so to walk,*n* even as he walked. *Ep. 5. 2. 1. P. 36. 13.*

7 Brethren, I write no new commandment unto you, but an old commandment, which ye had from the beginning. The old commandment is the word which ye have heard from the beginning.

8 Again, a new *o* commandment I write unto you; which thing is true in him and in you, because the darkness*p* is past, and the true light now shineth.

9 He that saith he is in the light, and hateth his brother, is in darkness *p* even until now.

10 He that loveth his brother abideth in the light, and there is none *y* occasion of stumbling in him.

11 But he that hateth his brother is in darkness, and walketh*u* in darkness, and knoweth not whither he goeth, because that darkness hath blinded his eyes.

12 I write unto you, little children, because your sins are forgiven you for his name's*y* sake. *Ph. 3. 9. Ep. 4. 32, 33.*

a Jno.1.1,&c.
b chap. 1. 1.
c 2 Pe. 1. 16.
d Lu. 24. 39.
e Jno.14.7,9.
f Jno.17.3.
g Ep. 6. 10.
h John 15. 7.
i Re. 2. 7, &c.
k Ro. 12. 2.
l John 17. 21.
m Mat. 6. 24.
Ga. 4. 4.
Ja. 4. 4.
n John 15. 11.
o 2 Pe. 2. 10.
p Ps. 119. 37.
q Ps. 73. 6.
r John 1. 4, 9.
1 Ti. 6. 16.
s Ps. 39. 6.
1 Co. 7. 31.
t John 12. 35.
u He. 1. 2.
w Mat. 24. 24.
1 Ti. 4. 1.
x Ep. 1. 7.
He. 9. 14.
1 Pe. 1. 19.
Re. 1. 5.
y 1 Ki. 8. 46.
Job 25. 4.
Ec. 7. 20.
Ja. 3, 2.
z Job 33. 27,
28.

Ps. 32. 5.
Pr. 28. 13.
a 2 Ti. 2. 19.
b Ps. 51. 2.
1 Co. 6. 11.
c 2 Ti. 3. 9.
d 2 Co. 1. 21.
e 1 Co. 2. 15.
f Ro. 8. 34.
He. 7. 25.
g Ro. 3. 25.
h chap. 4. 3.
i John 15. 23.
k Lu. 6. 46.
John 14. 15,
23.
l 2 John 6.
m John 15.4,5.
n John 13.15.
o John 17.3.
p John 13. 26.
q John 13.34.
r Ro. 13. 12.
8 or, it.
s 2 Pe. 1. 9.
γ scandal.
8 or, know ye.
t Je. 13. 23.
Mat. 7. 16..
18.
u Pr. 4. 25,
John 12. 35.
v Ep. 2. 4, 5.
w John 1. 12.
Re. 21. 7.
x John 17. 25.
y Ps. 25. 11.
Lu. 24. 47.
Ac. 10. 43.
z Ro. 8.14,18.

173

13 I write unto you, fathers, because ye have known him *b* that is from the beginning. I write unto you, young men, because ye have overcome the wicked one. I write unto you, little children, because ye have known the Father.*c*

14 I have written unto you, fathers, because ye have known him that is from the beginning. I have written unto you, young men, because ye are strong,*g* and the word of God abideth *k* in you, and ye have overcome *i* the wicked one.

15 Love *k* not the world, neither the things that are in the world. If *m* any man love the world, the love of the Father is not in him.

16 For all that is in the world, the lust *c* of the flesh,*o* and the lust of the *p* eyes, and the pride *q* of life, is not of the Father, but is of the world.

17 And *i* the world passeth away, and the lust thereof: but he that doeth the will of God abideth for ever.

18 Little children, it is the last *u* time: and as ye have heard *w* that antichrist shall come, even now are there many antichrists; whereby we know that it is the last time.

19 They went out from us, but they were not of us; for *a* if they had been of us, they would no doubt have continued with us: but they went out, that they might be made manifest *c* that they were not all of us.

20 But ye have an unction *d* from the Holy One, and ye know *e* all things.

21 I have not written unto you because ye know not the truth, but because ye know it, and that no lie is of the truth.

22 Who is a liar, but he that *h* denieth that Jesus is the Christ? He is antichrist, that denieth the Father and the Son.

23 Whosoever *i* denieth the Son, the same hath not the Father: [but] he that acknowledgeth the Son, hath the Father also.

24 Let *i* that therefore abide *m* in you, which ye have heard from the beginning. If that which ye have heard from the beginning shall remain in you, ye also shall continue in the Son, and in the Father.

25 And this is the promise that he hath promised us, even eternal *o* life.

26 These things have I written unto you concerning them that seduce you.

27 But the anointing which ye have *q* received of him abideth in you, and ye *r* need not that any man teach you: but as the same anointing teacheth*p* you of all things, and is truth, and is no lie, and even as it hath taught you, ye shall abide in *p* him.

28 And now, little children, abide in him; that, when he shall appear, we may have confidence, and not be ashamed before him at his coming.

29 If ye know that he is righteous, ye know that *t* every one that doeth righteousness is born of him.

CHAPTER III.

BEHOLD, what manner of love *v* the Father hath bestowed upon us, that we should be called the sons*w* of God; therefore the world *x* knoweth us not, because it knew him not.

2 Beloved, now are we the sons*z* of

ξ Ex. 20. 20. c. 3. 6, 9. 6c 20. 6   II Ge. 137.
Jo. 5. 14, — 5. 18.   I P. 4. 1.
— 8. 11   P. 4. 4.   Jo. 8. 34, 36.
He. 12. 1 — 34. 1.   I Go. 15. 34.
Is. 5. 21.   114. 31. Jude 5. 24.

One Hour with Jesus.

————

"What! could ye not watch with Me one hour?"

————

A N echo of this utterance of pathetic surprise, this wonderfully gentle reproof, seems to float around a matter of daily experience, and, with too many, of daily faithlessness. Our Divine Master has called us to no Gethsemane-watch of strange and mysterious darkness. It is while the brightness of day is breaking—perhaps even long after it has broken—that His call to communion with Himself reaches our not always willing ear. "Come with me!" (Song of Solomon 4:8). And the drowsy reply too often is, "Presently, Lord! not just this minute!"

And then, after "yet a little sleep, a little slumber, a little folding of the hands to sleep," the precious hour is past which "might have been" so full of blessing.

"What! could ye not watch with Me one hour?"

What is the practical answer of very many of His disciples?

"Oh, *yes!* very easily and readily, when the 'one hour' is at night, and we do not feel particularly inclined to go to bed, especially if we have a nice fire to 'watch' by. But oh, *no!* if the 'one hour' involves getting up at seven instead of eight, especially on a cold and gloomy morning. *That* is a very different matter!"

Were the question asked, "What one thing do you suppose has most hindered the largest number of Christians this day and this year in their spiritual life and growth?" I should reply unhesitatingly, "Probably the temptation not to rise in time to put on their armour as well as their dress before breakfast."

A mere ten minutes—is that enough preparation for our warfare and provision for our wants; for spreading all our needs and difficulties before the Lord; for telling Jesus all that is in our hearts; for bringing before Him all the details of our work; for searching to know His mind and His will; for storing His word in our hearts; for replenishing our seed-baskets, that we may have something to sow, and getting Him to sharpen our sickles that we may reap; for confession and supplication and intercession, and, above all, for *praise?*

Ten minutes or a quarter of an hour! Is that enough for the many things which He has to say unto us? for the quiet teachings of His Spirit, for the dawning of His light on the dark sayings of old, and the flashing of His glory and power on the words which are spirit and life? Is that enough to spend in converse with the Friend of friends? Does this look as if we really cared very much about Him? Even if it were enough for our small, cool affection, is it enough, think you, for His great love? enough to satisfy the Heart that is waiting to commune with ours? He loves us so much that He will have us with Him forever, and we love Him so little that we did not care to turn out of bed this morning in time to have even half-an-hour of real intercourse with Him. For it would have been "with Him." There was no doubt about His being at the tryst. He slumbered not; "He faileth not"—but we failed. What have we missed this morning! How do we know what He may have had to say to us? What have we missed all the mornings of this past year!

"But it comes to the same thing if I go up-stairs after breakfast!" *Does* it "come to the same thing"? You know perfectly, and by repeated experience, that it *does not.* Letters and newspapers have come; you stay to read them, you must just see what So-and-so says, and what the telegrams are; and then you must just attend to sundry little duties, and then somebody wants you, and then you really ought to go out, and so perhaps you never "go up-stairs" at all. Or, if you do, perhaps your room is not "done," or you are interrupted or called down. Satan is astonishingly ingenious in defeating these good after-breakfast intentions. And yet these external devices are not his strongest. Suppose you do get away after breakfast without external hindrance or interruption, he has other moves to make. Do you not find that the "things which are seen" have got the start of the "things which are not seen"? not necessarily sinful things, but simply the "*other* things entering in" which are "not the things which are Jesus Christ's," yet they choke the word, and hinder prayer. You have an unsettled feeling; you do not feel sure you will not be wanted or interrupted; it is an effort—pretty often an unsuccessful one—to forget the news, public or private, which has come by post; bits of breakfast table-talk come back to mind; voices or sounds in the now stirring household distract you; you ought, you know you ought, to be doing something else at that hour, unless, indeed, you are a drone in the home-hive, or willfully "out of work" as to the Lord's vineyard. And so it does *not* "come to the same thing" at all, but you go forth ungirded to the race, unarmed to the warfare. What marvel if faintness and failure are the order of the day!

I suppose there is not one of us who has not made "good resolutions" about this, and—broken them. And this is not very surprising, considering that "good resolutions" are never mentioned in the Bible as any item of armour or weapons for "the good fight of faith." So let us try something better.

First, *Purpose.* This is what we want; neither languid and lazy wishing, nor fitful and impulsive resolving, but calm and humble and steady purpose, like David's (Psalm 17:3), Daniel's (Daniel 1:8), and St. Paul's (2 Timothy 3:10). Without purpose, even prayer is paralyzed, and answer prevented. Now, have we any purpose in this matter? in other words, do we really *mean* to do what we say we wish to do? If not, let us ask at once that the grace of purpose may be wrought in us by the Spirit of all grace.

Secondly, *Prayer.* Having purposed by His grace, let us ask that our purpose may, also by His grace, be carried into effect. It will not do merely to lament and pray vaguely about it. To-morrow morning will not do; the thing must be done to-night. To-night, then, tell the gracious Master all about it, tell Him of the past disloyalty and sin in this matter, so that you may go to the coming battle strong in the strength of His pardoning love and His cleansing blood, and His tenderly powerful "Go, and sin no more." Do not make a good resolution about all the mornings of your life—His way is "morning by morning" (Isaiah 50:4), and His way is best. Ask Him to give you the grace of energy for this one coming morning, if you are spared to see it. Ask Him to give you a holy night, that you may remember Him upon your bed, and that even the half-conscious moments may be full of Him. Ask Him that when you awake you may be "still with Him," and that He would then enable you unreluctantly to rise, eager and glad to watch with Him "one hour," uninterrupted and quiet, "alone with Jesus."

Even Prayer and Purpose may be neutralized by want of—

Thirdly, *Self-denying Forethought.* We almost make the difficulty for ourselves when we forget that we can not burn a candle at both ends. If we *will* sit up at night, of course we make it harder in proportion to get up in the morning. "I would give anything to be able to get this precious 'one hour'!" says a lie-a-bed Christian, or one who really needs a long night's sleep. No! there is one thing you will not give for it, and that is an hour of your pleasant evenings. It is too much to expect you to leave the cosy fireside, or the delightful book, or the lively circle an hour earlier, so that you may go to bed in good time, and be more ready to rise in the morning. No; you could not really be expected to include *that* in the "anything" you are ready to give for the true "early communion" with your Lord. And yet only try it, and see if the blessing is not a hundredfold more than the little sacrifice.

Perhaps we hardly need say that the habit of reading any ordinary book after we go up-stairs, "only just a few pages, you know," is simply fatal to the sweet and sacred "one hour," whether that night or next morning. Oh, let your own room at any rate be sacred to the One Blessed Guest! Do not keep Him waiting, because you "wanted just to finish a chapter" of any book but His own. Finishing one chapter too often leads to beginning another, and to filling the mind with "other things." And then, "Dear me, I had no idea it was so late!" And, all the while, the King was waiting! What wonder that you find the audience chamber closed, when you at last put down your book!

Will not this be enough? Not quite. Not even Purpose and Prayer and Self-denying Forethought are enough without—

Fourthly, *Trust*. Here is the joint in the harness, the breaking-down point. Praying, and not trusting Him to answer; putting on other pieces of armour, and not covering them all with the shield of faith; asking Him to do something for us, and then not entrusting ourselves to Him to have it done for us. Distrusting one's self is one thing; distrusting Jesus is quite another. No matter at all, nay, so much the better that you feel, "I have failed morning after morning; I am at my wits' end; I can not summon resolution, when the moment comes, to jump up; it is no use making resolutions, I only break them again and again!" Only, do not stop there. "I *can't*, but Jesus *can!*" will settle this, and everything else.

"I *can't* make myself get up, therefore—*i.e.*, just *because* I can't—I will put it into my Lord's hands, and trust Him to make me get up. He will undertake for me even in this." One feels humbled and ashamed to be reduced to this, and rightly enough; it proves how despicably weak we are. The apparent smallness of the trial enhances the greatness of the failure. It adds new force to "Without Me ye can do nothing," when conscience whispers, "Exactly so! nothing! not even get out of bed at the right moment!"

But it is when we have come to this point, and see that all the strength of ourselves and our resolutions *is* utter weakness, that we see there is nothing for it but to say, "Jesus, I will trust *Thee!*" Say that to Him to-night with reference to this often lost battle. Trust, simply and really *trust*, Him to win it for you, and you will see that He will not disappoint your trust. He NEVER does! The secret of success is trust in Him who "faileth not," and learning this secret in this one thing, may and should lead you to trust, and therefore to succeed, in many another battle. For—

> "From victory to victory
> His army shall be led."

But what about His suffering ones, His physically weak ones, who can not or must not rise early? How glad we are that the true reason or motive is "opened unto the eyes of Him with whom we have to do," the High-Priest who is "touched with the feeling of our infirmities!" He knows these cases, and, "in some way or other, the Lord will provide"; His grace will be sufficient, and that which is spiritual loss, if arising from our own indolence, will be turned into spiritual gain if arising from His accepted chastening. I think our dear Master will see to it that these shall not be losers; He will give opportunity, and grace to take it; He can even give quietness and communion amid the mid-day surroundings. Still, unquestionably, special watchfulness and special grace are needed, when, through ill-health, the usual early hour can not be secured.

These may surely take all the comfort of His most gracious words, "The spirit indeed is willing, but the flesh is weak." They are never to be perverted into excuse for sinful indolence; and it is never to be allowed that our Lord could have spoken excusingly of that flesh figurative, which is to be crucified, mortified, reckoned dead, given no quarter whatever. But they are gracious indeed, as referring to this literal mortal flesh in which the life of Jesus is to be made manifest, the body of which He is the Saviour, the frame which He tenderly "remembereth." Many a mistake arises from confusing these two distinct meanings of the word.

Some who are not invalids, have yet great difficulties, owing to household arrangements over which they have no control. Since these thoughts were first printed, I have received so many touching letters from younger or dependent members of Christian households, that I can not refuse to insert a loving appeal to my senior friends not to hinder any under their roofs in this most important matter. A late or uncertain hour for evening prayers is a more serious hindrance to young or delicate persons, or those who have had a busy day, than they imagine. "They do not like me to leave the room before prayers; and afterwards I am so tired that I really *can't* enjoy my Bible as I wish." If "*they*" only knew how the stereotyped domestic arrangements are hindering the grace of God in the heart of daughter, visitor, governess, or servant, surely, oh, surely! it would not be thought too great a sacrifice to "have prayers a little earlier." At *least,* no hindrance by word, or even look, should be placed in the way of any one's slipping away earlier in the evening, for a little time alone with Him *before* they are "too tired," and returning when the bell rings for family worship. Then retiring *immediately* to rest, the inestimable "one hour" in the morning need not be lost through physical weariness which a little kind consideration might avoid. In this matter—

> Evil is wrought by want of thought,
> As well as want of heart.

Let us not forget, but remember in grateful contrast, how many there are who have to be hard at work before our earliest thoughts of rising; to whom "an hour earlier" would be a physical impossibility, the long day's work being followed by unpeaceful evenings in the noisy dwellings of noisy alleys. No quiet for them till long after we are in our quiet rooms; the short interval between the latest sounds of drunkenness and the inexorable factory-bell being perhaps still further shortened by a long distance to walk. And no quiet corner to retire to, no possibility of kneeling "*alone* with Jesus," at any time of day or night! Will not some who thus have to seek Him "in the press," rise up in judgment against us who may have an undisturbed hour alone with Him every morning, if we will?

The following testimony is from one of England's most successful and eminent men of business. He writes:—

"In the busy life I have lived, I owe much to the practice of very early rising to secure the 'hour with Jesus' which you recommend. Even now, I find very early rising essential to the maintenance of spiritual life and close communion with God; and being now somewhat weak physically, nothing but the *desire* for this communion is sufficient to enable me to rise.

"My wife rises about 6, remaining in her room till 8, or she would not, with her large household, be equal, spiritually, to her duties."

Is not this one of the many "new leaves" which onward-pressing pilgrims should desire to turn over with the New Year? And will it not be the truest means of ensuring a Happy New Year? Happier, brighter, holier, more useful and more victorious; more radiant with His Presence and more full of His Power than any previous one.

The time past of our lives may surely suffice us for the neglect of this entirely personal and entirely precious privilege. We have suffered loss enough;—shall we not henceforth, "from this time," seek the gain, the spiritual wealth which this "one hour" will assuredly bring? Cold mornings! well, the good Master who knoweth our frame and its natural shrinking from "His cold" knows all about them. But was there ever an added difficulty for which He could not and would not give added strength and "more grace"? So do not let us wait for the summer mornings which may never be ours to spend in earthly communion, nor even for the childish idea of making a special start on New Year's Day.

When we are "called" *to-morrow* morning, let it remind us of her who "called Mary her sister, saying, The Master is come, and calleth for thee." For

He will certainly be there, waiting for us. What will you do? We know what Mary did. "*As soon as* she heard that, she arose quickly, and came unto Him."

Please see Robert Murray M'Cheyne's *Calendar for reading through the Word of God in a year* at the end of this book, pages 64–91.

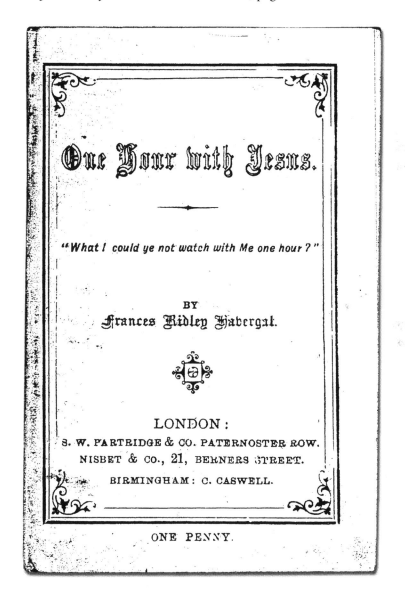

Frances Ridley Havergal wrote in a letter to a friend,

> "Now tell me whether you have seen *Hints on Bible-marking*, by
> Mrs. Stephen Menzies, because, if you have not, I will send it to you.
> The plan was not new to me, but I am *very* glad it is issued—chiefly
> thanks to Moody.
> "Does not His Word open out more and more, as the years go on?
> One feels greedy of every bit that one seems to get hold of for oneself. I
> so often look forward and wonder, 'What next, Lord? what will be the
> next unexpected shining upon a text, or golden thread put into one's
> hand to string many upon?'" [1]

F.R.H. used this system in her own Bible study, and her personal Bagster
study Bible has her underlinings, "railroadings," and references. If the Lord will,
an Addendum Facsimile Edition of Havergal's Bagster Study Bible will be published with this edition of her *Complete Works*. She truly loved the Word of God:
the written Word, the Scriptures, His own and very words to us, and the Word
made flesh, the Lord Jesus Christ. She was intimately familiar with every page
of the Bible. Maria wrote in *Memorials of Frances Ridley Havergal* and *Lilies and
Shamrocks* that F.R.H. memorized all the New Testament except the Book of
Acts, all the Minor Prophets, Isaiah, and all the Psalms. (Maria would not have
overstated any more than Frances, and sooner understated, leaving out books
not completely memorized and chapters learned.) She read with serious profi-
ciency, diligence, love, the original Hebrew and Greek texts. Maria wrote in her
biography *Memorials* about Frances' study in her last eight months, when she
lived with Maria in Swansea, Wales:

> It was at her study table that she read her Bible by seven o'clock in
> the summer and eight o'clock in winter; her Hebrew Bible, Greek Tes-
> tament, and lexicons being at hand. Sometimes, on bitterly cold morn-
> ings, I begged that she would read with her feet comfortably to the fire,
> and received the reply: "But then, Marie, I can't rule my lines neatly;
> just see what a find I've got! If one only searches, there are such extraor-
> dinary things in the Bible!" [2]

---

[1] *Letters by the Late Frances Ridley Havergal* edited by her sister, Maria V. G. Havergal (London: James Nisbet & Co., 1886), original page 155, page 190 of Volume IV of the Havergal
edition, Division IV, the third letter to "M.F."

[2] *Memorials of Frances Ridley Havergal* by Maria V. G. Havergal (London: James Nisbet &
Co., 1880), original page 259, page 69 of Volume IV of the Havergal edition, Chapter XIII.

HINTS

ON

BIBLE MARKING.

BY

MRS. STEPHEN MENZIES.

PREFATORY NOTE

BY

D. L. MOODY.

LONDON:

SAMUEL BAGSTER AND SONS ;

15, PATERNOSTER ROW.

Price Sixpence.

PREFATORY NOTE.

It gives me the greatest pleasure to add my testimony to the value of this plan of Bible Marking. In these days when the very foundations of truth are assailed, we have but one refuge—the precious, unchangeable Word of God. I conceive that we can scarcely be engaged in any service more useful, than in endeavouring to facilitate and deepen the study of the Bible.

I believe the suggestions in the following plan will not only interest *young* Christians, but will also help *more advanced* believers, already engaged in Bible teaching; inasmuch as this plan of Bible Marking, with the insertion of Side Notes, Marginal References, etc., converts the margins of one's Bible into a note-book ready to hand at any moment.

I heartily trust the plan will be carefully studied and extensively used; and I doubt not but that here in this country, as in England, it will prove a great blessing.

D. L. MOODY,

Northfield, Mass., U.S.A.

November 9th, 1875.

HINTS
ON BIBLE MARKING.

The following plan of Bible Marking has for many years been pursued by some who have given themselves especially to searching into God's Word; and the practical result is, that it has proved a greater help than perhaps any other, to Bible study.

Its peculiar advantage consists in this: that it affords a means by which every fresh thought or idea may be committed to the pages of one's Bible, instead of to a Note-book. This is done, as will be seen from the following pages, either by "railways," or by marginal references, or by concise jottings in any spare corner of the page. As every new thought is gathered, it is at once committed to this safe repository. Thus one's Bible becomes enriched with these constant gleanings, and they are always at hand when studying or teaching.

The study of God's Word was perhaps never so much needed as at the present time. Hundreds of young converts throughout our land are rejoicing in their new-found peace. But what about their growth, their walk, their testimony? How can they *grow*, unless they feed? How can they walk "so as He walked," unless they behold *His* glory? How can they testify of things which they have never seen nor heard? It is of the very first importance that they should get to their Bibles. If we are to be strong *muscular* Christians, growing up into Christ in *all* things, it can only be as our thirst is quickened, and our love deepened, for the constant and prayerful study of the Word of God.

To *young* Christians in particular, it is believed, the following Plan will be of the greatest service, stimulating to a deeper search, and supplying a means of retaining all that is gained.

One objection *only* has ever been raised against this method: *viz.*, the peculiar appearance which the pages present when crossed by the "railways." When *properly* marked, however, and the lines drawn with a fine pen, they are but little observed; and the practical utility is *so* great, that to this, one gladly sacrifices the mere appearance.

The following Specimen Pages are from BAGSTER's Bible, which excels all other Bibles on account of its Facsimile Editions. But the same Plan can be followed out on any Bible with *almost* equal facility.

It is proposed to issue Monthly a Leaflet giving new "Railways," references, and jottings *upon this Plan*, which may be added to one's Bible. This little Paper will be entitled, "FRAGMENTS THAT REMAIN" (*Price 1d. Postage extra*); and may be obtained on the first of each month, from

Mrs. Stephen Menzies, Eccleston Hill, St. Helens, Lancashire.

EXPLANATIONS.

The horizontal lines under the words, are called *Underlines*; and the diagonal lines are termed "Railways."

Underline the word or words with which a "Railway" is to be connected.

In any given verse, underline *only* the word or words required to convey the thought; leaving other words to be underlined in connection with other thoughts which may occur hereafter.

It often occurs that "Railways" are connected with two or three separate parts of one verse. This can only be expressed by carefully observing the above Rule.

The connection between an underline and a "Railway" should always be made at one end of the underline, and not in the middle of an underline.

Draw the "Railways" on each page as nearly as possible at the same angle; by so doing the print will be far less interfered with. See page 158 where the "Railways" over verses 10, 12, 14, 15, 17 are very nearly at the same angle. Observe where this rule is infringed, verse 18.

A "Railway" continued into the Margin and ended with a *letter* or number, indicates that a similar continuation, with a corresponding letter or number, will be found elsewhere on the same page (though it may be in the other column).

If a connection be needed with a *distant* page, the same is indicated by continuing the "Railway" into the Margin, and writing at the end of the "Railway" the chapter and verse with which it is connected. See page 47, Luke 8. 50.

A "Railway" may often be useful to connect a verse with a group of jottings, or foot-notes. See top of page 57, Ex. 28. 1. Also page 158, Heb. 2. 17.

Never draw "Railways" without a Small Ruler, and a fine Etching pen; and be very careful that the underlines and the "Railways" are drawn accurately.

Draw lines as lightly as possible, particularly the "Railways."

Make your own Marginal references as freely as possible, writing each verse against the other. Thus:—

Heb. 2. 11=Ex. 25. 19: write Heb. 2. 11 beside Ex. 25. 19; and Ex. 25. 19 beside Heb. 2. 11.

In all jottings or "Notes," be very concise, so as to occupy little space.

Further hints as to the arrangement of lines, "Railways," etc., will be more easily gathered by a careful study of the following pages, than by fuller written explanations.

SIGNS AND ABBREVIATIONS.

⊙ signifies the new Rendering according to Alford.

✳ signifies a Foot-note or Head-note.

△ signifies "Trinity."

Ctr. signifies Contrast.

Cf. signifies Compare.

Mat. Behold a King shall reign.
Mᵏ. Behold my Servant.
Lu. Behold the Man.
Jno. Behold the Lamb of God.

Conversions
Andrew.
Simon.
Philip.
Nathanael.
Woman of Samaria.
Nicodemus.
Blind man.

7 Gifts in John
His flesh   6 . 51
His life   10 : 11
Example   13 : 15
Comforter   14 : 16
My peace   14 : 27
His words   17 : 8
His Glory   17 : 22

The GOSPEL according to St. JOHN.

Jesus "the Word" 1 : 1v
John "the Voice" 1 : 23v

Key Verse Chap. 16 : 28

15 Titles of Christ in ch. 1

Key Words give
loved.
ch. 3 : 16 believed.
life.

CHAPTER I.

A. D. 26.

IN@ the beginning was the Word, and the Word was with God, and the Word was God.

2 The same was in the beginning with God.

3 All things were made by him; and without him was not any thing made that was made.

4 In him was life; and the life was the light of men.

5 And the light shineth in darkness; and the darkness comprehended it not.

6 There was a man sent from God, whose name was John.

7 The same came for a witness, to bear witness of the Light, that all men through him might believe.

8 He was not that Light, but was sent to bear witness of that Light.

9 That was the true Light, which lighteth every man that cometh into the world.

10 He was in the world, and the world was made by him, and the world knew him not.

11 He came unto his own, and his own received him not.

12 But as many as received him, to them gave he power to become the sons of God, even to them that believe on his name:

13 Which were born, not of blood, nor of the will of the flesh, nor of the will of man, but of God.

14 And the Word was made flesh, and dwelt among us, (and we beheld his glory, the glory as of the only begotten of the Father,) full of grace and truth.

15 John bare witness of him, and cried, saying, This was he of whom I spake, He that cometh after me is preferred before me: for he was before me.

16 And of his fulness have all we received, and grace for grace.

17 For the law was given by Moses, but grace and truth came by Jesus Christ.

18 No man hath seen God at any time; the only begotten Son, which is in the bosom of the Father, he hath declared him.

19 And this is the record of John, when the Jews sent priests and Levites from Jerusalem to ask him, Who art thou?

20 And he confessed, and denied not; but confessed, I am not the Christ.

21 And they asked him, What then? Art thou Elias? And he saith, I am not. Art thou that prophet? And he answered, No.

22 Then said they unto him, Who art thou? that we may give an answer to them that sent us. What sayest thou of thyself?

23 He said, I am the voice of one crying in the wilderness, Make straight the way of the Lord, as said the prophet Esaias.

24 And they which were sent were of the Pharisees.

25 And they asked him, and said unto him, Why baptizest thou then, if thou be not that Christ, nor Elias, neither that prophet?

26 John answered them, saying, I baptize with water: but there standeth one among you, whom ye know not;

27 He it is, who coming after me is preferred before me, whose shoe's latchet I am not worthy to unloose.

28 These things were done in Bethabara beyond Jordan, where John was baptizing.

29 The next day John seeth Jesus coming unto him, and saith, Behold the Lamb of God, which taketh away the sin of the world.

30 This is he of whom I said, After me cometh a man which is preferred before me: for he was before me.

31 And I knew him not: but that he should be made manifest to Israel, therefore am I come baptizing with water.

32 And John bare record, saying, I saw the Spirit descending from heaven like a dove, and it abode upon him.

33 And I knew him not: but he that sent me to baptize with water, the same said unto me, Upon whom thou shalt see the Spirit descending, and remaining on him, the same is he which baptizeth with the Holy Ghost.

34 And I saw, and bare record that this is the Son of God.

35 Again the next day after John stood, and two of his disciples;

36 And looking upon Jesus as he walked, he saith, Behold the Lamb of God!

37 And the two disciples heard him speak, and they followed Jesus.

38 Then Jesus turned, and saw them following, and saith unto them, What seek ye? They said unto him, Rabbi, (which is to say, being interpreted, Master,) where dwellest thou?

39 He saith unto them, Come and see. They came and saw where he dwelt, and abode with him that day: for it was about the tenth hour.

40 One of the two which heard John speak, and followed him, was Andrew, Simon Peter's brother.

41 He first findeth his own brother Simon, and saith unto him, We have found the Messias, which is, being interpreted, the Christ.

42 And he brought him to Jesus. And when Jesus beheld him, he said, Thou art Simon the son of Jona: thou shalt be called Cephas, which is by interpretation, A stone.

43 The day following Jesus would go forth into Galilee, and findeth Philip, and saith unto him, Follow me.

44 Now Philip was of Bethsaida, the city of Andrew and Peter.

45 Philip findeth Nathanael, and saith unto him, We have found him, of whom Moses in the law, and the prophets, did write, Jesus of Nazareth, the son of Joseph.

46 And Nathanael said unto him, Can there any good thing come out of Nazareth? Philip saith unto him, Come and see.

47 Jesus saw Nathanael coming to him, and saith of him, Behold an Israelite indeed, in whom is no guile!

48 Nathanael saith unto him, Whence knowest thou me? Jesus answered and said unto him, Before that Philip called thee, when thou wast under the fig tree, I saw thee.

49 Nathanael answered and saith unto

ch. 1. 49 "King of Israel".
ch. 1. 51. "Son of Man".

64

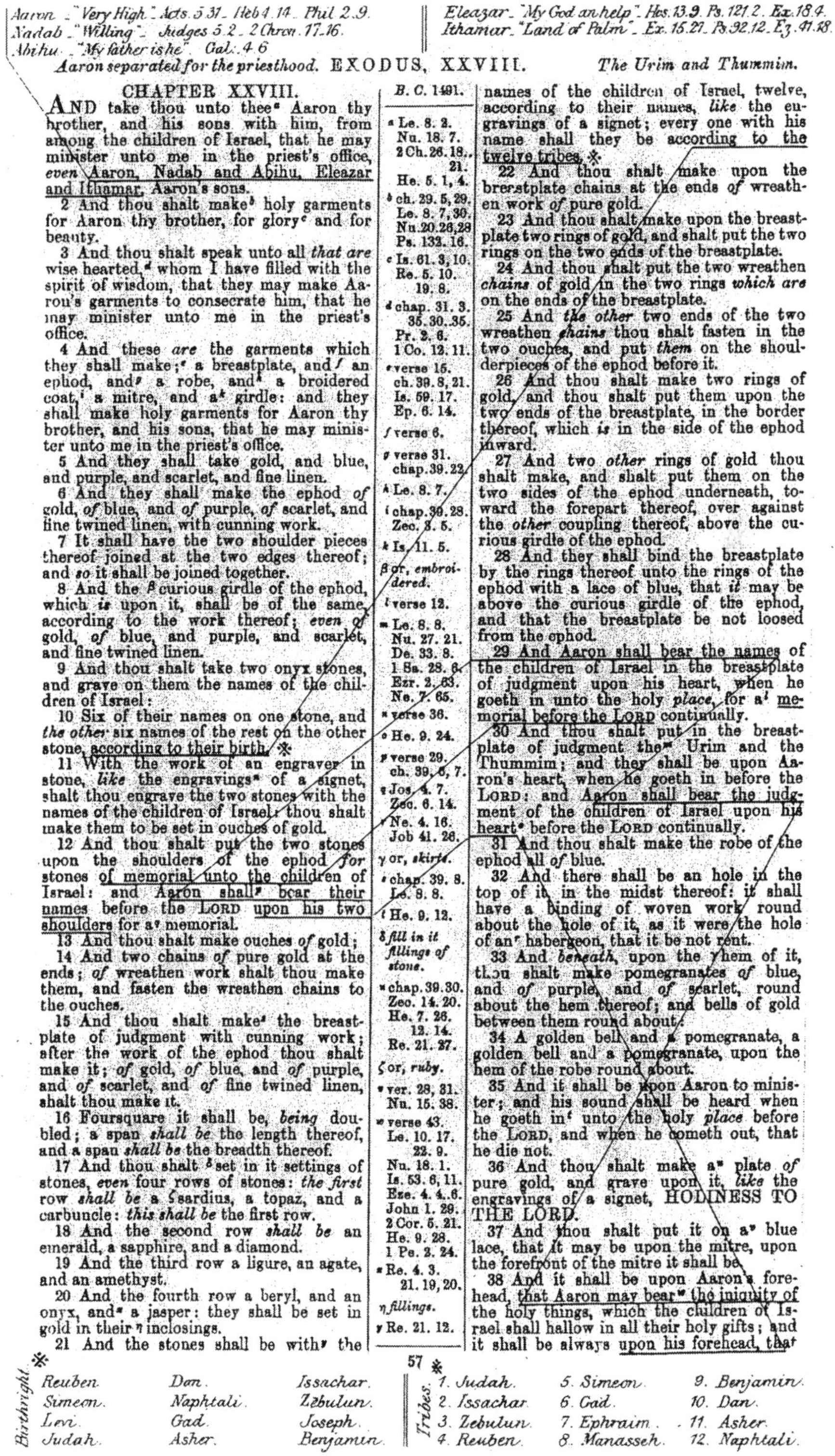

Aaron – "Very High" – Acts 5.31 – Heb 4.14 – Phil 2.9.
Nadab – "Willing" – Judges 5.2 – 2 Chron. 17.16.
Abihu – "My father is he" – Gal. 4.6
Eleazar – "My God an help" – Hos. 13.9. Ps. 121.2. Ex. 18.4.
Ithamar – "Land of Palm" – Ex. 15.27 – Ps. 92.12 – Ez. 41.18.

Aaron separated for the priesthood. EXODUS, XXVIII. *The Urim and Thummim.*

CHAPTER XXVIII.

AND take thou unto thee[a] Aaron thy
brother, and his sons with him, from
among the children of Israel, that he may
minister unto me in the priest's office,
even Aaron, Nadab and Abihu, Eleazar
and Ithamar, Aaron's sons.
2 And thou shalt make[b] holy garments
for Aaron thy brother, for glory[c] and for
beauty.
3 And thou shalt speak unto all *that are*
wise hearted,[d] whom I have filled with the
spirit of wisdom, that they may make Aaron's garments to consecrate him, that he
may minister unto me in the priest's
office.
4 And these *are* the garments which
they shall make;[e] a breastplate, and[f] an
ephod, and[g] a robe, and[h] a broidered
coat,[i] a mitre, and a[k] girdle: and they
shall make holy garments for Aaron thy
brother, and his sons, that he may minister unto me in the priest's office.
5 And they shall take gold, and blue,
and purple, and scarlet, and fine linen.
6 And they shall make the ephod *of*
gold, *of* blue, and *of* purple, *of* scarlet, and
fine twined linen, with cunning work.
7 It shall have the two shoulder pieces
thereof joined at the two edges thereof;
and *so* it shall be joined together.
8 And the [β]curious girdle of the ephod,
which *is* upon it, shall be of the same,
according to the work thereof; *even of*
gold, *of* blue, and purple, and scarlet,
and fine twined linen.
9 And thou shalt take two onyx stones,
and grave on them the names of the children of Israel:
10 Six of their names on one stone, and
the other six names of the rest on the other
stone, according to their birth. ※
11 With the work of an engraver in
stone, *like* the engravings[n] of a signet,
shalt thou engrave the two stones with the
names of the children of Israel: thou shalt
make them to be set in ouches of gold.
12 And thou shalt put the two stones
upon the shoulders of the ephod *for*
stones of memorial unto the children of
Israel: and Aaron shall[p] bear their
names before the LORD upon his two
shoulders for a[q] memorial.
13 And thou shalt make ouches *of* gold;
14 And two chains *of* pure gold at the
ends; *of* wreathen work shalt thou make
them, and fasten the wreathen chains to
the ouches.
15 And thou shalt make[s] the breastplate of judgment with cunning work;
after the work of the ephod thou shalt
make it; *of* gold, *of* blue, and *of* purple,
and *of* scarlet, and *of* fine twined linen,
shalt thou make it.
16 Foursquare it shall be, *being* dou-
bled; a span *shall be* the length thereof,
and a span *shall be* the breadth thereof.
17 And thou shalt [δ]set in it settings of
stones, *even* four rows of stones: *the first*
row *shall be* a [ζ]sardius, a topaz, and a
carbuncle: *this shall be* the first row.
18 And the second row *shall be* an
emerald, a sapphire, and a diamond.
19 And the third row a ligure, an agate,
and an amethyst.
20 And the fourth row a beryl, and an
onyx, and[x] a jasper: they shall be set in
gold in their [η]inclosings.
21 And the stones shall be with[y] the

B. C. 1491.

[a] Le. 8. 2. Nu. 18. 7. 2 Ch. 26. 18, 21. He. 5. 1, 4.
[b] ch. 29. 5, 29. Le. 8. 7, 30. Nu. 20. 26, 28. Ps. 132. 16.
[c] Is. 61. 3, 10. Re. 5. 10. 19. 8.
[d] chap. 31. 3. 35. 30..35. Pr. 2. 6. 1 Co. 12. 11.
[e] verse 15. ch. 39. 8, 21. Is. 59. 17. Ep. 6. 14.
[f] verse 6.
[g] verse 31. chap. 39. 22.
[h] Le. 8. 7.
[i] chap. 39. 28. Zec. 3. 5.
[k] Is. 11. 5.
[β] or, *embroidered.*
[l] verse 12.
[m] Le. 8. 8. Nu. 27. 21. De. 33. 8. 1 Sa. 28. 6. Ezr. 2. 63. Ne. 7. 65.
[n] verse 36.
[o] He. 9. 24.
[p] verse 29. ch. 39. 6, 7.
[q] Jos. 4. 7. Zec. 6. 14.
[r] Ne. 4. 16. Job 41. 26.
[γ] or, *skirts.*
[s] chap. 39. 8. Le. 8. 8.
[t] He. 9. 12.
[δ] *fill in it fillings of stone.*
[u] chap. 39. 30. Zec. 14. 20. He. 7. 26. 12. 14. Re. 21. 27.
[ζ] or, *ruby.*
[v] ver. 28, 31. Nu. 15. 38.
[w] verse 43. Le. 10. 17. 22. 9. Nu. 18. 1. Is. 53. 6, 11. Eze. 4. 4..6. John 1. 29. 2 Cor. 5. 21. He. 9. 28. 1 Pe. 2. 24.
[x] Re. 4. 3. 21. 19, 20.
[η] *fillings.*
[y] Re. 21. 12.

names of the children of Israel, twelve,
according to their names, *like* the engravings of a signet; every one with his
name shall they be according to the
twelve tribes. ※
22 And thou shalt make upon the
breastplate chains at the ends *of* wreath-
en work *of* pure gold.
23 And thou shalt make upon the breastplate two rings of gold, and shalt put the two
rings on the two ends of the breastplate.
24 And thou shalt put the two wreathen
chains of gold in the two rings *which are*
on the ends of the breastplate.
25 And *the other* two ends of the two
wreathen *chains* thou shalt fasten in the
two ouches, and put *them* on the shoul-
derpieces of the ephod before it.
26 And thou shalt make two rings of
gold, and thou shalt put them upon the
two ends of the breastplate, in the border
thereof, which *is* in the side of the ephod
inward.
27 And two *other* rings of gold thou
shalt make, and shalt put them on the
two sides of the ephod underneath, toward the forepart thereof, over against
the *other* coupling thereof, above the curious girdle of the ephod.
28 And they shall bind the breastplate
by the rings thereof unto the rings of the
ephod with a lace of blue, that *it* may be
above the curious girdle of the ephod,
and that the breastplate be not loosed
from the ephod.
29 And Aaron shall bear the names of
the children of Israel in the breastplate
of judgment upon his heart, when he
goeth in unto the holy *place*, for a[l] memorial before the LORD continually.
30 And thou shalt put in the breastplate of judgment the[m] Urim and the
Thummim; and they shall be upon Aaron's heart, when he goeth in before the
LORD: and Aaron shall bear the judgment of the children of Israel upon his
heart[o] before the LORD continually.
31 And thou shalt make the robe of the
ephod all *of* blue.
32 And there shall be an hole in the
top of it, in the midst thereof: it shall
have a binding of woven work round
about the hole of it, as it were the hole
of an[r] habergeon, that it be not rent.
33 And *beneath*, upon the [γ]hem of it,
thou shalt make pomegranates *of* blue,
and *of* purple, and *of* scarlet, round
about the hem thereof; and bells of gold
between them round about:
34 A golden bell and a pomegranate, a
golden bell and a pomegranate, upon the
hem of the robe round about.
35 And it shall be upon Aaron to minister: and his sound shall be heard when
he goeth in[t] unto the holy *place* before
the LORD, and when he cometh out, that
he die not.
36 And thou shalt make a[u] plate *of*
pure gold, and grave upon it, *like* the
engravings of a signet, HOLINESS TO
THE LORD.
37 And thou shalt put it on a[v] blue
lace, that it may be upon the mitre, upon
the forefront of the mitre it shall be.
38 And it shall be upon Aaron's forehead, that Aaron may bear[w] the iniquity of
the holy things, which the children of Israel shall hallow in all their holy gifts; and
it shall be always upon his forehead, that

57

※ Birthright.

Reuben.	Dan.	Issachar.
Simeon.	Naphtali.	Zebulun.
Levi.	Gad.	Joseph.
Judah.	Asher.	Benjamin.

※ Tribes.

1. Judah.	5. Simeon.	9. Benjamin.
2. Issachar.	6. Gad.	10. Dan.
3. Zebulun.	7. Ephraim.	11. Asher.
4. Reuben.	8. Manasseh.	12. Naphtali.

Faith	"Kept by"	Faith in Exercise
Source of faith Ep.2.8	The Father 1 Pet.1.5	Obeying Rom. 16.26
Object Heb.12.2	The Son Jno. 10.28	Living Gal. 2.20
Ground Rom.10.11	The Spirit Is. 59.19	Walking 2Cor. 5.7
Righteousness Rom.4.13		Working 1Thes. 1.3
Unity Ep.4.13		Praying Jas. 5.15
Trial 1Pt.1.7		Enduring 1Pet. 1.7
✱ End of 1Pet.1.9		Fighting 1 Tim.6.12

The First Epistle general of PETER.

Pilgrims, Strangers, Priests here — glory, there.

CHAPTER I.

PETER, an apostle of Jesus Christ, to the strangers scattered[b] throughout Pontus, Galatia, Cappadocia, Asia, and Bithynia,

2 Elect[c] according to the foreknowledge[d] of God the Father, through sanctification[e] of the Spirit, unto[f] obedience and sprinkling[g] of the blood of Jesus Christ: Grace unto you, and peace, be multiplied.[i]

3 Blessed[k] be the God and Father of our Lord Jesus Christ, which according to his[5] abundant[m] mercy hath begotten us again[n] unto a (lively) hope by the resurrection[p] of Jesus Christ from the dead,

4 To an inheritance[q] incorruptible, and undefiled, and that fadeth[r] not away, reserved[8] in heaven for[7] you,

5 Who are kept[8] by the power of God through faith[u] unto salvation, ready to be revealed in the last time.

6 Wherein ye greatly rejoice, though now for a season, if need[v] be, ye are in heaviness through manifold temptations:

7 That the (trial[x]) of your faith, being much more precious than of gold that perisheth, though it be tried with[c] fire, might be found unto praise and[d] honour and glory at the appearing[e] of Jesus Christ:

8 Whom having not[f] seen, ye love; in whom, though now ye see him not, yet believing, ye rejoice with joy unspeakable and full of glory:

9 Receiving the end of your faith, even the salvation of your souls. ⊙

10 Of which salvation the prophets have inquired and searched[m] diligently, who prophesied of the grace that should come unto you:

11 Searching what, or what manner of time the Spirit[p] of Christ which was in them did signify, when it testified beforehand the sufferings of Christ, and the glory that should follow.

12 Unto whom it was revealed, that not[t] unto themselves, but unto us they did minister the things, which are now reported unto you by them that have preached the gospel unto you with the Holy Ghost[w] sent down from heaven; which things the angels[x] desire to look into.

13 Wherefore gird[z] up the loins of your mind, be sober,[a] and hope[9] to the end[c] for the grace that is to be brought unto you at the revelation of Jesus Christ;

14 As obedient children, not fashioning[3] yourselves according to the former lusts in your ignorance:

15 But as he which hath called you is holy, so be ye[5] holy in all manner of conversation:

16 Because it is written,[c] Be ye holy; for I am holy.

17 And if ye call on the Father, who without respect of persons judgeth ac-

A.D. 60.

a Phi. 2. 12.
b Ac. 8. 4.
c Ep. 1. 4.
d Ro. 8. 29.
e 2 Th. 2. 13.
f Ro. 16. 26.
g He. 12. 24.
h Jno.1.29,36
Re. 7. 14.
i Jude 2.
k 2 Co. 1. 3.
l Re. 13. 8.
β much.
m Ep. 2. 4.
n John 3.3,5.
o Mat. 28.18.
Phi. 2. 9.
p 1 Co.15.20.
q He. 9. 15.
r Jno.17.17,19
t Col. 1. 5.
γ or, us.
u 1Jno.3.14,16
Jude 1. 24.
x Ep. 2. 8.
y John 1. 13.
x He.12.7..11.
z Ja. 1. 18.
δ or, For that.
a Is. 40. 6..8.
b Ja. 1. 3, 12.
c 1 Co. 3. 13.
d Ro. 2. 7,10.
e Ro. 1. 7.
f John1.1,14.
2 Pe. 1. 19.
g 1John 4.20.
h Ep. 4. 23,31.
i John 16. 22.
k Mat. 18. 3.
l 1 Co. 3. 2.
m Da. 9. 3.
n Ps. 34. 8.
o Ps. 118. 22.
p 2 Pe. 1. 21.
ζ or, be ye.
q He. 3. 6.
r Is. 61. 6.
Re. 1. 6.
s Mal. 1. 11.
t He.11.39,40
u Is. 28. 16.
v 2 Co. 4. 2.
w Ep. 3. 10.
η or, an honour.
x Lu. 12. 35.
y Mat. 21. 42.
z Lu. 21. 34.
θ perfectly.
a He. 10. 35.
b Ro. 12. 2.
c Jude 4.
κ or, purchased.
d De. 4. 20.
λ or, virtues.
e Le. 11. 44.
f Ac. 26..18.
g Ro. 9. 25.

cording to every man's work, pass the time of your sojourning here in fear:[e]

18 Forasmuch as ye know that ye were not redeemed with corruptible things, as silver and gold, from your vain conversation received by tradition from your fathers;

19 But with the precious blood of Christ, as of a lamb[h] without blemish and without spot: → Ex.12.5. 2.Pt.3.14

20 Who verily was foreordained before[i] the foundation of the world, but was manifest in these last times for you;

21 Who by him do believe in God, that raised[m] him up from the dead, and[o] gave him[n] glory; that your faith and hope might be in God.

22 Seeing ye have purified your souls in obeying the truth[q] through the Spirit unto unfeigned love[u] of the brethren, see, Jno.13.35 that ye love one another with a pure heart fervently:

23 Being born[y] again, not of corruptible seed, but of incorruptible, by the word[z] of God, which liveth and abideth for ever.

24 [δ]For[a] all flesh is as grass, and all the glory of man as the flower of grass. The grass withereth, and the flower thereof falleth away:

25 But the word of the Lord endureth Mat.24.35 for ever. And this[f] is the word which by the gospel is preached unto you.

CHAPTER II.

WHEREFORE laying aside[h] all malice, Ep.4.22 and all guile, and hypocrisies, and envies, and all evil speakings,

2 As newborn babes,[k] desire the sincere milk[l] of the word, that ye may grow thereby: 2 Pet. 3.18

3 If so be ye have tasted[n] that the Lord is gracious.

4 To whom coming, as unto a living stone, disallowed[o] indeed of men, but chosen of God and precious.

5 Ye also, as lively stones,[s] are built Ep.2.21 up a spiritual house,[t] an holy priesthood,[r] to offer up spiritual[t] sacrifices, acceptable to God by Jesus Christ.

6 Wherefore also it is contained in the scripture,[u] Behold, I lay in Sion a chief corner stone, elect, precious: and he that believeth on him shall not be confounded.

7 Unto you therefore which believe he is precious: but unto them which be Hs.119 disobedient, the stone[y] which the builders disallowed, the same is made the head of the corner,

8 And a stone of stumbling, and a rock of offence, even to them which stumble at the word, being disobedient: whereunto[c] also they were appointed.

9 But ye are a chosen generation, a Ex.19.6 royal priesthood, an holy nation, a [κ]peculiar[d] people; that ye should shew forth the [λ]praises of him who hath called 2Cor.3.3 you out of darkness[f] into his marvellous light:

10 Which[g] in time past were not a people, but are now the people of God;
→ 2 Pet. 1.1

168

God-ward	Balance of Truth	Man-ward	
Justified by Faith	Romans	Justified by Works	James
Sanctified by Christ 1Cor.1.2		Sanctified by the Spirit	Gal.1. 2.
Accepted in---	Ep.1.6	Accepted of Him	2Cor.5.9
We are Source	2Thn.2.19	Depart from iniquity	2Tim.2.19
Kept	1Pt.1.5	Keep yourselves	Jude.21
Builded	Ep.2.22	Building up	Jude.20
Clean	Jno.13.10	Cleanse yourselves	2Cor.7.1

Joy	unspeakable	1Pet.1.8
Gift	unspeakable	2Cor.9.15
Riches	unsearchable	Ep.3.8
Judgments	unsearchable	Rom.11.33
Ways	past finding out	Rom.11.33
Peace	passing understanding	Phil. 4.7
Love	passing knowledge	Ep.3.19

"In Love"	Walk	Our Inheritance	His Inheritance	7 Togethers	Heirship		
Ch. 1. 4	Ch.2:2,10	Salvation ..Heb 1:14	Saints ..Ep.1:18	Quickened ..Ch:2:5	Basis of H'ship .Sonship	..Gal. 4.7.
. 3.17	. 4.1	Promise ...6.17	Heathen ..Ps:2:8	Raised ..Ch:2.6	Giver . The Father	..Deu. 26.1
. 1:2	. 4.17	Right of Faith .11:7	Israel ..Deut 4:20	Seated ..Ch:2.6	Partner . The Son	..Rom:8:17
. 4.15	. 5.2	Hope ...Tit.3:7	All Things ..Heb:1:2	Planted ..Rom6:5	Earnest . The Spirit	.Ep:1.14.
. 4.16	. 5. 8	Grace of Life 1Pet.3:7		Sufferers ..Rom 8:17	Condition. Suffering	..Rom.8.17
. 5 2	. 5.15	Kingdom .Jas. 2:5		Heirs Rom.8:17	Nature . Incorrupt..	1Pet:1.4.
		God ...Gal 4:7		Glorified ..Rom.8:17	Scene . The Glory	.Col:1.12

The Epistle of PAUL the Apostle to the EPHESIANS.

Jesus _ Jehovah.
Christ . or Messiah . Anointed.
Jesus Christ . As living & dying on earth
Christ Jesus . Risen & Ascended
J.C. our Lord . Having purchased us
C.J our Lord - Having Sealed & Anointed us with His Spirit

"Sit" "Walk" "Stand"
Chps 1&2 4 & 3 6.

Keyword "In" from heaven

dead in Sins. Ep:2.
death for Sin . 1Pet.:2.
dead to Sin . Rom:6.

CHAPTER I.

A.D. 64.

PAUL, an apostle of Jesus Christ by the will of God, to the saints b which are at Ephesus,c and to the faithful d in Christ Jesus:

2 Grace f be to you, and peace from God our Father, and from the Lord Jesus Christ.

3 Blessed h be the God and Father of our Lord Jesus Christ, who hath blessed us with all spiritual blessings in heavenly γ places in Christ: →to Ch:3.11

4 According as he hath chosen j us in him before the foundation of the world, that we should be holy k and without blame before him in love:

Is.53:10 5 Having predestinated m us unto the adoption n of children by Jesus Christ to himself, according to the good pleasure p of his will,

Father 6 To the praise q of the glory of his grace, wherein he hath made us accepted r in the beloved?

Ex.12:43 7 In whom s we have redemption through his blood, the forgiveness of sins, according to the riches of his grace;

Lev.17.11 8 Wherein he hath abounded toward us in all wisdom and prudence;

9 Having made known unto us the mystery of his will, according to his good pleasure which he hath v purposed in himself:

Jno.11.52 10 That in the dispensation of the fulness of times, he might gather together in one all things in Christ, both which are in heaven, and which are on earth; even in him:

11 In whom also we have obtained an inheritance, being predestinated according to the purpose of him who worketh all things after the counsel of his own will;

Son. 12 That we might be to the praise of his glory, who first trusted in Christ.

13 In whom ye also trusted, after that ye heard the word of truth, the gospel of your salvation: in whom also, after that

Ac.11.17 ye believed, ye were sealed with that holy Spirit of promise, on believing

'H S' 14 Which is the earnest of our inheritance, until the redemption of the purchased possession, unto the praise of his glory. →redemption of appropriation

15 Wherefore I also, after I heard of your faith in the Lord Jesus, and love unto all the saints,

16 Cease not to give thanks for you, making mention of you in my prayers;

Ac 7.2 17 That the God of our Lord Jesus Christ, the Father of glory, may give unto you the spirit of wisdom and revelation in the knowledge of him:

18 The eyes of your understanding being enlightened; that ye may know what is the hope of his calling, and what

the riches a of the glory of his inheritance in the saints,

19 And what is the exceeding greatness of his power e to us-ward who believe, according to the working of his β mighty power.

20 Which he wrought in Christ, when he r raised him from the dead, and set him at his own right hand in the heavenly places,

21 Far i above all principality, and power, and might, and dominion, and every name that is named, not only in this world, but also in that which is to come;

22 And hath put l all things under his feet, and gave him to be the head over all things to the church,

23 Which is his body,o the fulness of him that filleth all in all.)

CHAPTER II.

AND you hath he quickened, who were dead in trespasses and sins;

1Cor.6.11 2 Wherein in time past ye walked according to the course of this world, according to the prince of the power of

Phil.2:13 the air, the spirit that now worketh in the children of disobedience:

3 Among whom also we all had our living (conversation) in times past in the lusts of our flesh, fulfilling the desires of the flesh and of the mind; and were by nature the children of wrath, even as others. Phil 3:20

4 But God, who is rich in mercy, for his great love wherewith he loved us,

1Pet 2.24 5 Even when we were dead in sins, hath quickened us together with Christ, (by grace ye are saved;) have been

6 And hath raised us up together, and made us sit together in heavenly places in Col.3:1 Christ Jesus:

7 That in the ages to come he might shew the exceeding riches of his grace, in his Ch:3.16 kindness toward us through Christ Jesus.

8 For by grace are ye saved through faith; and that not of yourselves: it is the gift of God: →have ye been-

9 Not of works, lest any man should boast. 2 Tim. 1. 9.10

10 For we are his workmanship, created in Christ Jesus unto good works, which Ex 28.33 God hath before ordained that we should walk in them.

11 Wherefore remember, that ye being in time past Gentiles in the flesh, who are called Uncircumcision by that which is called the Circumcision in the flesh made by hands;

12 That at that time ye were without Christ, being aliens from the commonwealth of Israel, and strangers from the covenants of promise, having no hope, and without God in the world:

13 But now, in Christ Jesus, ye who aforetime sometimes were far off, are made nigh by the blood of Christ. without Christ without God no hope

a chap. 3. 16.
b Ro. 1. 7.
c Ac. XIX. XX.
d Col. 1. 2.
e Ps. 110. 3.
β the might of his power.
f Ga. 1. 3.
Tit. 1. 4.
g Ac. 2.24,33.
h 2 Co. 1. 3.
1 Pe. 1. 3.
i Phi. 2. 9.
Col. 2. 10.
γ or, things,
He. 9. 23.
j 1 Pe. 1. 2.
k Lu. 1. 75.
Col. 1. 22.
l Ps. 8. 6.
Mat. 28. 18.
m Ro. 8.29,30.
n John 1. 12.
o 1 Co. 12. 12.
Col.1.18,24.
p Lu. 12. 32.
q 1 Pe. 2. 9.
r John 5. 24.
Col. 2. 13.
s 1 Pe. 2. 5.
t Ac. 19. 35.
u He. 9. 12.
1 Pe.1.18,19
v chap. 6. 12.
w Col. 3. 6.
x 1 Pe. 4. 3.
δ wills.
y 2 Ti. 1. 9.
z Ps. 51. 5.
a Ro.5,6,8,10.
ζ the heavens.
η by whose.
b Ro. 3. 24.
c Col. 2. 12.
d Ac. 20. 32.
e Tit. 3. 4.
f 2 Ti. 1. 9.
g Ro. 4. 16.
h Jno.6. 44,65.
θ or, hoped.
i Ro. 10. 17.
k 2 Co. 1. 22.
l 2 Co. 5. 5.
m Ro. 8. 23.
n chap. 1. 4.
κ prepared.
o Ac. 20. 28.
p ver. 6, 12.
q John 20. 17.
r Col. 1. 9.
λ or, for the acknowledgment.
s Is. 42. 7.
t chap. 4. 4.
κ He. 9. 12.

137

△ See verses 6, 12, 14.

The calling of the Gentiles. EPHESIANS, III. Unity of the Christian faith.

14 For he *a* is our peace, who hath made both *d* one, and hath broken down the middle wall of partition between us;

Cd.2.M.D. 15 Having abolished *f* in his flesh the enmity, even the law of commandments contained in ordinances; for to make in himself of twain one new man, so making peace;

16 And that he might reconcile *i* both unto God in one body by the cross, having slain the enmity *β* thereby; *⊙ glad tidings d*

Lu 2:10 17 And came and preached *peace* to
Re.10.15 you *l* which were afar off, and to them
Ac.13.32 that were nigh. *Heb. 4. 2.*

△ 18 For through *n* him we both have access by one Spirit unto the Father.

Heb.2.11 19 Now therefore ye are no more strangers and foreigners, but fellowcitizens *o* with the saints, and of the household *p* of God;

20 And are built *q* upon the *r* foundation of the apostles and prophets, Jesus Christ
Is. 28.16 himself being the chief *t* corner *stone;*

21 In whom all the building, fitly framed together, groweth unto an holy *v* temple in the Lord : *being builded ⊙*

△ 22 In whom ye also are *u* builded *w* together for an habitation of God through the Spirit.

CHAPTER III.

Co heirs FOR this cause I Paul, the prisoner of
Co members Jesus Christ for you Gentiles,
Co partners 2 If ye have heard of the dispensation *x* of the grace *y* of God, which is given me to you-ward :

3 How that by revelation *a* he made known unto me the mystery ; (as I wrote *b* afore in few words,

4 Whereby, when ye read, ye may understand my knowledge in the mystery *c* of Christ;)

5 Which in other ages was not *d* made known unto the sons of men, as it is now revealed unto his holy apostles and prophets by the Spirit ; *are.*

Co heirs 6 That the Gentiles (should be) fellow-
Co members heirs, and of the same body, and partakers
Co partners of his promise in Christ by the gospel ;

7 Whereof I was made a minister, according to the gift of the grace of God given unto me by the effectual *f* working of his power.

8 Unto me, who am less *h* than the least
Glad of all saints, is this grace given, that I
tidings should preach among the Gentiles the
of the unsearchable riches *k* of Christ : *verse 19*

9 And to make all men see, what is the fellowship of the mystery, *l* which from the beginning of the world hath been hid in God, who created all things by *n* Jesus Christ :

10 To the intent that now unto the principalities and powers in heavenly *places* might be known, by the church, the manifold wisdom *o* of God,

11 According to the *eternal* purpose
Ch.1.3. which he purposed in Christ Jesus our Lord :

12 In whom we have boldness *l* and access with confidence by the faith of him.

13 Wherefore I desire that ye faint not at my tribulations for you, which *u* is your glory.

14 For this cause I bow my knees unto the Father of our Lord Jesus Christ,

15 Of whom the whole family in heaven and earth is named,

16 That he would grant you, according

Paul's growth in grace

to the riches *b* of his glory, to be *c* strengthened with might by his Spirit in the inner man ; *d*

17 That Christ may dwell *f* in your hearts by faith ; that ye, being *k* rooted and grounded in love,

18 May be able to comprehend with all saints, what is the breadth, and length, and depth, and height ;

19 And to know the love of Christ, *Phil 4:7* which passeth knowledge, that ye might *2 Cr. 9:15* be filled with all the fulness *t* of God. *Cd.2:9*

20 Now *m* unto him that is able to do ※ exceeding abundantly above all that we ask or think, according to the power that worketh in us, *Ch. 1:19*

21 Unto him be glory in the church by Christ Jesus, throughout all ages, world without end. Amen.) /

CHAPTER IV.

I THEREFORE, the prisoner *y* of the Lord, beseech you that ye walk *z* worthy of the vocation wherewith ye are called,

2 With all lowliness *u* and meekness, with longsuffering, forbearing one another in love ; *earnestly strive Heb.4.11.*

3 Endeavouring *y* to keep the unity of the Spirit in the bond of peace.

4 There is one body, and one Spirit, even as ye are called in one hope of your calling ;

5 One Lord, one faith, one baptism,

6 One God and Father of all, who is *7 Unities.* above all, and through all, and in you all.

7 But unto every one of us is given grace according to the measure *v* of the gift of Christ.

8 Wherefore he saith, *b* When he ascended up on high, he led *c* captivity captive, and gave gifts unto men.

9 (Now that he ascended, what is it but that he also descended first into the lower parts of the earth ?

10 He that descended is the same also that ascended up far above all heavens, that he might *f* fill all things.)

11 And *h* he gave some, apostles ; and some, prophets ; and some, evangelists ; and some, pastors and teachers ;

12 For the perfecting of the saints, for the work of the ministry, for the edifying of the body of Christ : *ministration Mk.9.41*

13 Till we all come *f* in the unity *v* of the faith, and of the knowledge of the Son of God, unto a perfect *i* man, unto the measure of the stature *k* of the fulness of Christ :

14 That we henceforth be no more children, tossed to and fro, and carried *m* about with every wind of doctrine, by the sleight of men, and cunning craftiness whereby they lie in wait to deceive ;

15 But, *h* speaking the truth *m* in love, may grow up into him in all things, which is the head, *p* even Christ :

16 From whom *q* the whole body fitly joined together, and compacted by that *1 Cor.12.23* to the effectual working in the measure of every part, maketh increase of the body unto the edifying of itself in love.

17 This I say therefore, and testify in the Lord, that ye henceforth walk not as other Gentiles walk, in the vanity of their mind,

18 Having the understanding *s* darkened, being alienated from the life of God through the ignorance that is in them, because of the *u* blindness of their heart

Able.

A.D. 64.
a Mi. 5. 5.
b Phi. 4. 19.
c chap. 6. 10. Col. 1. 11.
d John 10. 16. Ga. 3. 28.
e Ro. 7. 22.
f Col. 2. 14.
g chap. 2. 22. John 14. 23.
h Col. 2. 7.
i Col. 1. 20..22
β or, in himself.
k John 1. 16.
l Ac. 2. 39.
m Ro. 16. 25. He. 13. 20.
21.
Jude 24.
n John 14. 6.
1 Pe. 3. 18.
o He. 12. 22,
23.
p chap. 3. 15.
q 1 Co. 3. 9,10.
r Mat. 16. 18. Re. 21. 14.
γ or, in.
s Col. 1. 10.
t Is. 28. 16.
u Mat. 11. 29.
v 1 Co. 3. 17. 2 Co. 6. 16.
w 1 Pe. 2. 4, 5.
x Col. 1. 25.
y Ro. 12. 3.
z Ro. 12. 3.
a Ga. 1. 12.
b Ps. 68. 18.
δ or, a little before.
ζ or, a multitude of captives.
c chap. 1. 9.
d Mat. 13. 17. Ro. 16. 25. 1Pe.1.10..12
η or, fulfil.
e 1 Co. 12. 28.
f chap. 1. 19. Is. 43. 13.
θ or, into.
g Col. 2. 2.
h 1 Co. 15. 9.
i 1 Co. 14. 20.
κ or, age.
k Col. 1. 27.
l ver. 4, 5. 1 Ti. 3. 16.
m Ja. 1. 6.
n Ps. 33. 6. John 1. 3. Col. 1. 16. He. 1. 2.
λ or, being sincere.
o 2 Co. 4. 2.
p Col.1.18,19.
q Ro. 11. 33. 1 Co. 2. 7.
r John 15. 5.
s chap. 1. 9.
t He. 4. 16.
u 2 Co. 1. 6.
v Ac. 26. 18.
μ or, hardness.

133 ※

A.D. 59. Least of the Apostles. 1 Cor. 15.9.
A.D. 61. Less than the least of all Saints. Ep. 3.8
A.D. 65. Chief of Sinners. 1Tim.1.15.

2 Cor. 9. 8   Rom. 4. 21
Jude   20   Rom. 14. 4
Heb. 2. 18   Acts. 20. 32
Heb. 7. 25   2 Tim. 1. 12
Phil. 3. 21   Ep. 3. 20
Mat. 9. 28 ?

ch.1.2. Better than Angels.	Heir of all things	1.2.
. 3. " Moses	Capt of our Salvation	11.10.
. 4. " Joshua	Apostle	3.1.
. 7. " Aaron	Author of Salvation	5.9.
	Fore runner	6.20.
	High Priest	10.21.
	All & Fin of Faith	12.2.

"Once"

ch. 9.7	Better Testament	7.22
. 9.12	Promises	8.6
. " 26	Substance	10.34
. " 27	Hope	7.19
. " 28	Sacrifices	9.23
. 10.2	Country	11.16
. " 10	Resurrection	11.35.

The Epistle of PAUL the Apostle to the HEBREWS.

— The Epistle of contrasts —   — Key Word — "Better" —

Christ on the throne having purged sin
Son of God

His people associated with Him
Son of Man.

CHAPTER I.

GOD, who *a* at sundry times and in divers manners, spake in time past unto the fathers by the prophets,

Verses 2.&.3
2 Hath in these last days spoken *b* unto us by *his* Son, whom he hath appointed *Christ's made the worlds:—Creator*
7 fold office
heir *d* of all things, by whom *e* also he made the worlds:—Creator 3 Who *f* being the brightness of *his* glory, and the express image of *his* person, and upholding all things by the word of his power, when he *g* had by himself purged *our* sins, sat down *h* on the right hand of the Majesty on high; *mediator*
4 Being made so much better than the angels, as he hath by inheritance obtained a more excellent name than they.

5 For unto which of the angels said he at *Resurr any time*, Thou *i* art my Son, this day have I begotten thee? And again, I *m* will be to *Ascension* him a Father, and he shall be to me a Son?
6 *And* again, when he bringeth in the *Coming Glory* firstbegotten into the world, he saith, And let all the angels of God worship him.
7 And *of* the angels he saith, Who maketh his angels spirits, and his ministers a flame of fire.
8 But unto the Son *he saith*, Thy throne, O God, is for ever and ever: a sceptre of *righteousness is* the sceptre of thy kingdom:
9 Thou hast loved righteousness, and hated iniquity; therefore God, *even* thy God, hath anointed thee with the oil of gladness above thy fellows.
10 And, Thou, *a* Lord, in the beginning hast laid the foundation of the earth; and the heavens are the works of thine hands:
11 They shall perish; but thou remainest: and they all shall wax old as doth a garment;
12 And as a vesture shalt thou fold them *ch.13.8.* up, and they shall be changed: but thou art the same, and thy years shall not fail.
13 But to which of the angels said he at any time, Sit *f* on my right hand, until I make thine enemies thy footstool? *r Lu.22.43*
14 Are they not all *ministering spirits*, sent forth *k* to minister for them who shall be heirs *l* of salvation? *r ch.6.17.*

CHAPTER II.

THEREFORE we ought to give the more earnest heed to the things which we have heard, lest at any time we should *k* let *them* slip.
binding
2 For if the word spoken by angels *l* was (stedfast,) and every transgression *m* and disobedience received a just recompence of reward;
3 How shall we *n* escape, if we neglect so great salvation; which *o* at the first began to be spoken by the Lord, and was confirmed unto us by them that heard *him*;
4 God *p* also bearing *them* witness, both with signs and wonders, and with divers miracles, and *μ* gifts of the Holy Ghost, according to his own will?

	A. D. 64.	
	a Nu. 12. 6, 8.	
	b De. 18.,15.	
	c Ps. 8. 4, &c.	
	d Ps. 2. 8.	
	e John 1. 3.	
	β or, *a little while inferior to.*	
	f John 1. 14.	
	Col.1.15.,17.	
	g chap. 7. 27.	
	9.12..14.	
	h Ps. 110. 1.	
	Ep. 1.20,21.	
	i 1 Co. 15. 24.	
	k Phi. 2. 8, 9.	
	y or, *by.*	
	l Ps. 2. 7.	
	m Ac. 2. 33.	
	n 2 Sa. 7. 14.	
	o John 3. 16.	
	δ or, *when he bringeth again.*	
	p Lu.24.26,46.	
	q Ro. 11. 36.	
	r Ps. 97. 7.	
	ζ *unto.*	
	s Ps. 104. 4.	
	t Is. 55. 4.	
	u chap.5.8,9.	
	Lu. 1. 32.	
	v Ps. 45. 6, 7.	
	w John 17. 21.	
	η *rightness,*or, *straitness.*	
	x Ps. 22. 22.	
	y Ps. 18. 2.	
	Is. 12. 2.	
	z Is. 8. 18.	
	a Ps. 102. 25.	
	b Jno.17.6.,12	
	c Jno. 1. 14.	
	d 1 Co. 15.54.	
	e Lu. 1. 74.	
	f Ps. 110. 1.	
	θ *he taketh not hold of angels, but of the seed of Abraham he taketh hold.*	
	g Ps. 103. 21.	
	Da. 7. 10.	
	h Ge.19.15,16.	
	Ps. 34. 7.	
	i Ro. 8. 17.	
	k ch. 4. 15,16.	
	κ *run out, as leaking vessels.*	
	l Ac. 7. 53.	
	m Nu. 15. 31.	
	n chap.4.1,11.	
	o Mar. 1. 14.	
	p chap. 4. 14.	
	λ *made.* *cm.*	
	q Ac. 14. 3.	
	r Nu. 12. 7.	
	μ or, *distributions.*	

5 For unto the angels hath he not put in subjection the world to come, whereof we speak.
6 But one in a certain place testified, saying, What is man, *c* that thou art mindful of him? or the son of man, that thou visitest him?
7 Thou madest him β a little lower *past* than the angels; thou crownedst him with *pres.t* glory and honour, and didst set him over *future* the works of thy hands:
8 Thou hast put all things in subjection under his feet. For in that he put all in subjection under him, he left nothing *that is* not put under him. But now we *see* not yet all things put under him.
9 But we see Jesus, who *k* was made a little lower than the angels, *y* for the suffering of death, crowned *m* with glory and honour; that he *n* by the grace of God should taste death for every man.
10 For it became him, *p* for whom *q are* all things, and by whom *are* all things, in bringing many sons unto glory, to make the captain *t* of their salvation perfect *u* through sufferings. *author* ⊙ *Ch.5.9.*
11 For both he that sanctifieth and they *Ex 25.19.* who are sanctified, *are* all *w* of one: for which cause he is not ashamed to call them brethren;
12 Saying, I *x* will declare thy name unto my brethren; in the midst of the church will I sing praise unto thee.
13 And again, I *y* will put my trust in him. And again, Behold I *z* and the children which God *b* hath given me. ※
14 Forasmuch then as the children are partakers of flesh and blood, he *c* also himself likewise took part of the same; that through death *d* he might destroy *1 Jno.3.8.* him that had the power of death, that is, the devil;
15 And deliver them who through fear *e 1 Sam.17.51.* of death were all their lifetime subject to bondage. *Num.35.12.. Eph.4.8 . 1.Cor.15.55.*
16 For verily *θ* he took not on *him the nature of* angels; but he took on *him* the seed *g* of Abraham.
17 Wherefore in all things it behoved him to be made like unto *his* brethren, that he might be a merciful *k* and faithful high priest in things *pertaining* to God, to make reconciliation for the sins of the people.
18 For in that he himself hath suffered being tempted, he is able to succour them that are tempted. *Sevenfold object of Christ's death.*

CHAPTER III.

WHEREFORE, holy brethren, partakers of the heavenly calling, consider the Apostle and High Priest *p* of our ~~pro~~-⊙-fession, ~~Christ~~ Jesus;
2 Who was *λ*faithful to him that *λ* appointed him, as also Moses *r was faithful* in all his house.
3 For this *man* was counted worthy of more glory than Moses, inasmuch as he

158

※ *"I myself will be still relying on Him."*

※ verse 14 . World .
*   - 13 - Flesh .*
*   - 12 - Devil .*

Parable of the Sower.

※ Mat. 28 - 9
*   Mk. 7 - 25*
*   Lu. 7 - 38*
*   " 8 - 35 "at his feet" (?)*
*   " 10 - 39*
*   " 17 - 16   The issue of blood healed.*
Jno 11 - 32

LUKE, VIII.

A.D. 31.

12 Those by the way side are they that hear; then cometh the devil, and taketh away the word out of their hearts, lest they should believe and be saved.

13 They on the rock are they, which, when they hear, receive the word with joy; and these have no root, which for a while believe, and in time of temptation fall away.

14 And that which fell among thorns are they, which, when they have heard, go forth, and are choked with cares and riches and pleasures of this life, and bring no fruit to perfection.

15 But that on the good ground are they, which, in an honest and good heart, having heard the word, keep it, and bring forth fruit with patience.

16 No man, when he hath lighted a candle, covereth it with a vessel, or putteth it under a bed; but setteth it on a candlestick, that they which enter in may see the light.

17 For nothing is secret that shall not be made manifest; neither any thing hid that shall not be known and come abroad.

18 Take heed therefore how ye hear: for whosoever hath, to him shall be given; and whosoever hath not, from him shall be taken even that which he seemeth to have.

19 Then came to him his mother and his brethren, and could not come at him for the press.

20 And it was told him by certain, which said, Thy mother and thy brethren stand without, desiring to see thee.

21 And he answered and said unto them, My mother and my brethren are these which hear the word of God, and do it.

22 Now it came to pass on a certain day, that he went into a ship with his disciples: and he said unto them, Let us go over unto the other side of the lake. And they launched forth.

23 But as they sailed, he fell asleep: and there came down a storm of wind on the lake; and they were filled with water, and were in jeopardy.

24 And they came to him, and awoke him, saying, Master, master, we perish! Then he arose, and rebuked the wind and the raging of the water: and they ceased, and there was a calm.

25 And he said unto them, Where is your faith? And they, being afraid, wondered, saying one to another, What manner of man is this! for he commandeth even the winds and water, and they obey him.

26 And they arrived at the country of the Gadarenes, which is over against Galilee.

27 And when he went forth to land, there met him out of the city a certain man, which had devils long time, and ware no clothes, neither abode in any house, but in the tombs.

28 When he saw Jesus, he cried out, and fell down before him, and with a loud voice said, What have I to do with thee, Jesus, thou Son of God most high? I beseech thee, torment me not.

29 (For he had commanded the unclean spirit to come out of the man. For oftentimes it had caught him: and he was kept bound with chains and in fetters; and he brake the bands, and was driven of the devil into the wilderness.)

30 And Jesus asked him, saying, What is thy name? And he said, Legion: because many devils were entered into him.

31 And they besought him that he

would not command them to go out into the deep.

32 And there was there an herd of many swine feeding on the mountain: and they besought him that he would suffer them to enter into them: and he suffered them.

33 Then went the devils out of the man, and entered into the swine: and the herd ran violently down a steep place into the lake, and were choked.

34 When they that fed them saw what was done, they fled, and went and told it in the city and in the country.

35 Then they went out to see what was done; and came to Jesus, and found the man, out of whom the devils were departed, sitting at the feet of Jesus, clothed, and in his right mind: and they were afraid.

36 They also which saw it told them by what means he that was possessed of the devils was healed.

37 Then the whole multitude of the country of the Gadarenes round about besought him to depart from them; for they were taken with great fear: and he went up into the ship, and returned back again.

38 Now the man out of whom the devils were departed, besought him that he might be with him: but Jesus sent him away, saying,

39 Return to thine own house, and shew how great things God hath done unto thee. And he went his way, and published throughout the whole city how great things Jesus had done unto him.

40 And it came to pass, that, when Jesus was returned, the people gladly received him: for they were all waiting for him.

41 And, behold, there came a man named Jairus, and he was a ruler of the synagogue; and he fell down at Jesus' feet, and besought him that he would come into his house:

42 For he had one only daughter, about twelve years of age, and she lay a dying. But as he went, the people thronged him.

43 And a woman having an issue of blood twelve years, which had spent all her living upon physicians, neither could be healed of any,

44 Came behind him, and touched the border of his garment: and immediately her issue of blood stanched.

45 And Jesus said, Who touched me? When all denied, Peter, and they that were with him, said, Master, the multitude throng thee and press thee, and sayest thou, Who touched me?

46 And Jesus said, Somebody hath touched me: for I perceive that virtue is gone out of me.

47 And when the woman saw that she was not hid, she came trembling, and falling down before him, she declared unto him, before all the people, for what cause she had touched him, and how she was healed immediately.

48 And he said unto her, Daughter, be of good comfort: thy faith hath made thee whole; go in peace.

49 While he yet spake, there cometh one from the ruler of the synagogue's house, saying to him, Thy daughter is dead: trouble not the Master.

50 But when Jesus heard it, he answered him, saying, Fear not: believe only, and she shall be made whole.

51 And when he came into the house he suffered no man to go in, save Peter.

47

Lu. 8. 42 Jairus' daugh.   child. rich.   just dead: father besought, friends fell forth.
*   7. 12 Widow's son.   youth. poor,   burying.   mother asked not bier stopped.*
Jno 11. 11 Lazarus,   aged. medl air. stinketh: sister doubted. stone roll'd away.

Ps. 132 { i. 10. Servant's prayer.
{ ii. 16. Lord's answer — 7 Twills."

God the giver of prosperity.   PSALMS, CXXVII.—CXXXIV.   *God's choice of Zion.*

4 Turn again our captivity, O LORD, as the streams in the south.
5 They that sow in tears shall reap in joy.
6 He that goeth forth and weepeth, bearing precious seed, shall doubtless come again with rejoicing, bringing his sheaves with him.

PSALM CXXVII.
A Song of degrees for Solomon.

EXCEPT the LORD build the house, they labour in vain that build it; except the LORD keep the city, the watchman waketh but in vain.
2 It is vain for you to rise up early, to sit up late, to eat the bread of sorrows: for so he giveth his beloved sleep.
3 Lo, children are an heritage of the LORD: and the fruit of the womb is his reward.
4 As arrows are in the hand of a mighty man; so are children of the youth.
5 Happy is the man that hath his quiver full of them: they shall not be ashamed, but they shall speak with the enemies in the gate.

PSALM CXXVIII.
A Song of degrees.

BLESSED is every one that feareth the LORD; that walketh in his ways.
2 For thou shalt eat the labour of thine hands: happy shalt thou be, and it shall be well with thee.
3 Thy wife shall be as a fruitful vine by the sides of thine house: thy children like olive plants round about thy table.
4 Behold, that thus shall the man be blessed that feareth the LORD.
5 The LORD shall bless thee out of Zion: and thou shalt see the good of Jerusalem all the days of thy life.
6 Yea, thou shalt see thy children's children, and peace upon Israel.

PSALM CXXIX.
A Song of degrees.

MANY a time have they afflicted me from my youth, may Israel now say:
2 Many a time have they afflicted me from my youth; yet they have not prevailed against me.
3 The plowers plowed upon my back; they made long their furrows.
4 The LORD is righteous: he hath cut asunder the cords of the wicked.
5 Let them all be confounded and turned back that hate Zion.
6 Let them be as the grass upon the housetops, which withereth afore it groweth up;
7 Wherewith the mower filleth not his hand, nor he that bindeth sheaves his bosom.
8 Neither do they which go by say, The blessing of the LORD be upon you: we bless you in the name of the LORD.

PSALM CXXX.
A Song of degrees.

OUT of the depths have I cried unto thee, O LORD.
2 Lord, hear my voice; let thine ears be attentive to the voice of my supplications.
3 If thou, LORD, shouldest mark iniquities, O Lord, who shall stand?
4 But there is forgiveness with thee, that thou mayest be feared.
5 I wait for the LORD, my soul doth wait, and in his word do I hope.
6 My soul waiteth for the Lord more than they that watch for the morning; I say, more than they that watch for the morning.

a Ps. 71. 5.
Ro. 8. 24.
He. 10. 35.
b Je.31.9..14.
c Ps. 103. 8.
β or, singing.
d Mat. 1. 21.
γ or, seed basket.
e Ps. 30. 5.
δ walk.
ζ or, of, Ps. 72, title.
f 1 Co.3. 6, 7.
η wonderful, Job 42. 3.
θ that are builders of it in it.
κ my soul.
g Mat. 18. 3.
h Ge.3.17, 19.
λ from now.
i Ge. 33. 5. 1 Sa. 2. 5.
μ filled his quiver with.
k 2 Sa.7.1,&c.
ν or, subdue, Ps. 18. 47, or, destroy.
l Job 5. 4.
m Ps. 112. 1.
π habitations.
n Is. 3. 10.
o Eze. 19. 10.
p Ps. 122. 1.
q Ps. 99. 5.
r Ps. 144. 12.
s Ps. 78. 61.
t Ps. 134. 3.
u Is. 65. 14.
v Ge. 50. 23. Job 42. 16.
w Ps. 125. 5.
x 1 Ki. 8. 25.
ρ belly.
σ or, much.
y Ex.1.13,14. La. 1. 3.
z John 16. 33.
a Ps. 68. 16.
τ or, surely.
b 1 Co.16.22.
c Lu 1. 53.
d verse 9.
e Mat. 13. 6, 21.
φ or, candle.
f 2 Ch. 21.7.
g Ru. 2. 4.
χ even together.
h La. 3. 55. Jon. 2. 2.
i Ex.30.25,30
k 2 Ch. 6. 40.
l Ps. 143. 2. Ro.3.20..24.
m De. 4. 48.
n Ex. 34. 7. Da. 9. 9. Ro. 8. 1.
o Je. 33. 8, 9. 2 Ti. 2. 19.
ψ or, which watch unto the morning.

7 Let Israel hope in the LORD: for with the LORD there is mercy, and with him is plenteous redemption.
8 And he shall redeem Israel from all his iniquities.

PSALM CXXXI.
A Song of degrees of David.

LORD, my heart is not haughty, nor mine eyes lofty: neither do I exercise myself in great matters, or in things too high for me.
2 Surely I have behaved and quieted myself, as a child that is weaned of his mother: my soul is even as a weaned child.
3 Let Israel hope in the LORD, from henceforth and for ever.

PSALM CXXXII.
A Song of degrees.

LORD, remember David, and all his afflictions;
2 How he sware unto the LORD, and vowed unto the mighty God of Jacob;
3 Surely I will not come into the tabernacle of my house, nor go up into my bed;
4 I will not give sleep to mine eyes, or slumber to mine eyelids,
5 Until I find out a place for the LORD, an habitation for the mighty God of Jacob.
6 Lo, we heard of it at Ephratah; we found it in the fields of the wood.
7 We will go into his tabernacles; we will worship at his footstool.
8 Arise, O LORD, into thy rest; thou, and the ark of thy strength.
9 Let thy priests be clothed with righteousness; and let thy saints shout for joy.
10 For thy servant David's sake turn not away the face of thine anointed.
11 The LORD hath sworn in truth unto David; he will not turn from it, Of the fruit of thy body will I set upon thy throne.
12 If thy children will keep my covenant, and my testimony that I shall teach them, their children shall also sit upon thy throne for evermore.
13 For the LORD hath chosen Zion; he hath desired it for his habitation.
14 This is my rest for ever: here will I dwell; for I have desired it.   Is. 57. 15
15 I will abundantly bless her provision: I will satisfy her poor with bread.   Mk.8.8
16 I will also clothe her priests with salvation; and her saints shall shout aloud for joy.
17 There will I make the horn of David to bud: I have ordained a lamp for mine anointed.
18 His enemies will I clothe with shame; but upon himself shall his crown flourish.

PSALM CXXXIII.
A Song of degrees of David.

BEHOLD, how good and how pleasant it is for brethren to dwell together in unity!
2 It is like the precious ointment upon the head, that ran down upon the beard, even Aaron's beard; that went down to the skirts of his garments;
3 As the dew of Hermon, and as the dew that descended upon the mountains of Zion: for there the LORD commanded the blessing, even life for evermore.

PSALM CXXXIV.
A Song of degrees.

BEHOLD, bless ye the LORD, all ye servants of the LORD, which by night stand in the house of the LORD.

402

In F.R.H.'s desk after she died was a hand-written list of projects, "Work for 1879 'If the Lord will.'" One of the items was "'About Bible marking.' Magazine article"—not completed when she so unexpectedly soon died. The following brief piece was published in the magazine *The Christian* for Thursday, June 5, 1879 (two days after F.R.H.'s death, prepared before her death), page 11. Frances possibly or likely was the "correspondent" here.   David Chalkley

HINTS ON BIBLE READING.—A correspondent has sent the result of some years' experience in Bible-study, which contains some useful hints. We quote the methods recommended. There are three chief methods of studying Scripture—(1) reading, (2) searching, (3) meditating. The first may be done by reading a daily portion (and this should never be neglected)—noting any parallelisms and contrasts in the text, the connexion with the preceding chapter, and repetitions of a word or phrase. Or the plan of reading single books again and again, or of looking up the references to some particular subject, may be adopted. As a companion in searching the Bible, a Concordance is indispensable, and should be used methodically and carefully. And our correspondent has something to say in favour of the plans of Bible-marking and "chains of texts," and also advocates the employment of alliteration and other mnemonic aids. The latter, together with careful attention during study, and the exercise of memory, will help to store the mind with treasures of Biblical knowledge available at any time.

THE CHRISTIAN.

Thursday, June 5, 1879.]

11

HINTS ON BIBLE-READING.—A correspondent has sent the result of some years' experience in Bible-study, which contains some useful hints. We quote the methods recommended. There are three chief methods of studying Scripture—(1) reading, (2) searching, (3) meditating. The first may be done by reading a daily portion (and this should never be neglected)—noting any parallelisms and contrasts in the text, the connexion with the preceding chapter, and repetitions of a word or phrase. Or the plan of reading single books again and again, or of looking up the references to some particular subject, may be adopted. As a companion in searching the Bible, a Concordance is indispensable, and should be used methodically and carefully. And our correspondent has something to say in favour of the plans of Bible-marking and "chains of texts," and also advocates the employment of alliteration and other mnemonic aids. The latter, together with careful attention during study, and the exercise of memory, will help to store the mind with treasures of Biblical knowledge available at any time.

This may have been (I think likely was) Frances' rough draft or introduction to her article on Bible marking and study, or another's summation of a longer article or draft by her. We do not know.   D.C.

"Thy Word is Truth."

My Bible Study:

FOR THE

Sundays of the Year.

BY

F. R. HAVERGAL.

"All the lessons He shall send
Are the sweetest:
And His training in the end
Is completest."—*F. R. H.*

NEW YORK:

ANSON D. F. RANDOLPH & COMPANY,

38 WEST TWENTY-THIRD STREET.

Note: Rev. Bullock through Home Words Publishing Office in London published two editions of this book: one is a normally typeset, printed text of Havergal's words, and the other is a facsimile edition with exact copies of her handwritten post-cards. The assignment of the various Studies among the 52 weeks is different for each of these editions. Another edition, published by Anson D. F. Randolph in New York, is a regularly typeset, printed text, but the order of the Studies for the 52 weeks is identical to the order in the facsimile edition, and this edition was chosen to be printed here.

Though F.R.H. agreed to gather and finalize this book for publication, she died unexpectedly young, and the Bible study postcards she sent to the Bullock family were gathered, arranged, and published posthumously. Very likely or almost surely, if Frances had lived on and finished this, she would have given this book a very different title. In a list of "Work for 1879 'If the Lord will.'" found in her desk after she died, her next to last item listed was this: "Complete the series of Sunday morning Crumbs." This may have been—or likely was—this set of Bible studies. If so, her title for this book may have been *Sunday Morning Crumbs*. These are truly crumbs—and more than crumbs—from the King's own table, rich gleanings from His Word.   David Chalkley

---

TWENTY-SIXTH WEEK.

I FORGOT to put down your address. Also I found I counted the chapters wrong, and ought to have given you a text from the *Fourth*. Then I *intended* to have given you 1 Sam. *x.* 19, "*rejected* of *God* who *Himself* saved you "—with Isa. liii. 3; but now see the *Eleventh* is the chapter. So I send for March 30, 1 Sam. xi. 9. A Royal message and the result of its reception. *Promised help* for the day of need (Ps. l. 15); *simple belief* that the King would be as good as His word, able and willing to deliver when no other could (see v. 3); and *consequent gladness*. See the margin, "God's help" is also "deliverance," and both are included in "Salvation," (make a railway to verse 13). "Let us therefore," etc. Heb. iv. 16; Ps. lxx. 5. Connect Luke ii. 10, and Rom. x. 15. What higher ambition or joy can we have than to be "messengers of the King's" help? Interesting to compare 1 Sam. xxxi. 11, 13, showing grateful remembrance.

42

TWENTY-SEVENTH WEEK.

FOR Sunday, April 6. 1 Sam. xviii. 4. I don't know if I am right, but it seems to me that in the friendship with Jonathan David's typical character as "king" is left out of sight, and he here illustrates our relationship to the King's *Son*. Then this verse is an exquisite picture, Christ *stripping* Himself, Phil. ii. 7, and Jo. xiii. 4; "*the robe that* WAS *upon Him*," John xvii. 22; "*gave it to D.*" Isa. lxi. 10, Ez. xvi. 8, (*my* skirts) "Sword" connects Eph. vi. 17 with "*given*" in Jo. xvii. 14. "*Bow.*" See Job xxix. 20, margin "*changed*," just our weak bow changed for His strong one. Gen. xlix. 24, "*Girdle*," Isa. xi. 5, 1 Cor. i. 30; Rev. xvii. 14 (*faithful*). *Why* all this? "*Because* he loved him."

43

TWENTY-SEVENTH WEEK.

For Sunday Aft. 6. I Sam. 10. 4. I don't know if I am right, but it seems to me that in the friendship with Jonathan David's typical character as "King" is left out of sight, & he tell illustrates our relationship to the King's Son. Here this one is an exquisite picture — it stripping himself — Phil 2. 7 v 70. 13. 4. "the robe that was upon him" John 17. 22. "gave it to D". Isa. 61. 10. Zg. 16. 8 (My shirt) "Sword" connect Eph. 6. 17 with "given" in Jo. 17. 14. "Bow". see Job 29. 20. margin "changed", "just our made how changed for his strong one Jer. 44. 14 (faithful), "Girdle". Sgs. 11. 5. I Cor. 1. 30. Rev. 17. 14 (faithful) Why all this? — Because he loved him.

G.M.B.

"He traineth so
That we may shine for Him in this dark world;
And bear His standard dauntlessly unfurled:
That we may show
His praise by lives that mirror back His love,
His witnesses on earth, as He is ours above."

F. R. H.

"What wouldst thou be?
A blessing to each one surrounding me;
A chalice of dew to the weary heart,
A sunbeam of joy bidding sorrow depart;
In the storm-tossed vessel a beacon light,
A nightingale song in the darkest night,
A beckoning hand to a far-off goal,
An angel of love to each friendless soul:
Such would I be,
Oh that such happiness were for me!"

F. R. H.

Engraved by W. BALLINGALL. THE MUMBLES' LIGHTHOUSE, NEAR SWANSEA.

(From a Sketch by F. R. H., taken from the Mumbles' Head, in 1854.)

FRANCES RIDLEY HAVERGAL "fell asleep" at Caswell Bay Road, The Mumbles, 3rd June, 1879.

This was the original frontispiece of this book, taken from a landscape drawing by F.R.H.

Contents.

———

"Nearer now than we Think."

By B. M., Author of "Elijah and other Poems."[1]

"I have no respite: I must make a little lull in life."
(*Last letter, received May 16th,* 1879.)

S HE stood in the glorious shadow
   Of the Father's house of love,
But she saw not the shining threshold
   Where the Angel-Watchmen move;
She heard not their garments faintly stir
As they opened the golden gates for her.

She had toiled in the blessed Vineyard,
   And as she toiled she sang,
Till far through the sunny distance
   That sweetest music rang;
And her fellow-workers, far and near,
Gave thanks to God for her words of cheer.

We heard her sing in the dawning,
   When the mists hung low and chill;
In the heavy heat of the noontide
   Her clear voice cheered us still;
And when evening shadows were closing round,
We folded our hands to that tender sound.

And those who were watching at midnight,
   Watching in pain or fear,—
Heard oft in that sorrowful stillness
   One sweet voice ringing clear:
For God her Maker, her God and King,
Had given her songs in the night to sing.

---

[1] This was Barbara Miller McAndrew.

And the souls that were passing in silence
    To the River dreary and dim,
Heard, down by its desolate margin,
    A sweet voice sing of Him,
Who will welcome His children " one by one,"
To the smiling city beyond the sun.

Far off on the desert mountains
    To wandering souls it came,
That sound of a tender message,
    That pleading in Christ's dear Name;
It followed the sorrowful path they trod,
Till the wandering spirits were turned to God.

And she sang to the little children,
    Of the children's God and King;
When heart and voice were weary
    She sang unfaltering;
And her fervent spirit leapt to see
The little ones gather, sweet Lord, to Thee.

But at length she longed for a " respite,"
    To gather in silence, alone,
New strength for her mighty harvest,
    For the great work yet to be done;
She prayed for a "lull" in the labour of life,
A breathing space in the glorious strife,—

For only a little shadow
    From the red sun's fiery glow,
One hour's brief rest by the fountains
    Where the waters of comfort flow,
Where the flowers are blowing, so pale and sweet,
In the tender gloom by the Master's feet.

Yet,—could she have rested ever
    Where the cool soft shadows lie,
Whilst weary and faint in the noontide
    One soul went wandering by?—
Nay; one sad step on the dreary road
Would have troubled her heart as it leant on God:

So willing to toil and travel,
    To suffer and watch for all,
So near in heart to the Master,
    So eager to follow His call,—
She spent her soul in the service sweet,
And only in Death could rest at His feet.

So *this* is the needed respite,
    Her shadow from noonday sun
Falls dark, from the wing of the Angel,
    Who comes when our work is done,
To bring no " lull " in the hurry of life,
But the Conqueror's Rest after toil and strife.

And now in the King's own Palace,
    She sings to her harp of gold,
With the seal of God on her forehead,
    In her spirit His peace untold,
Where never a sorrowful step nor cry
Shall break on the lull of Eternity.

Introductory Note.

THE readers of " ROYAL BOUNTY" will remember a " Postscript " in which the gifted author urged very strongly the importance of the regular and systematic study of the Word of God. As a help to this end she commended to their notice THE CHRISTIAN PROGRESS SCRIPTURE READING AND PRAYER UNION,[1] the members of which agree to read the Old and New Testament, in arranged portions, daily, morning and evening, throughout the year. The advantages of this course of Bible reading in giving wide and balanced views of the great field of God's truth, as well as drawing closely in Christian fellowship the hearts of those who are thus led at one and the same time to pray and seek for Divine teaching, have approved themselves to many thousands; amongst whom " F. R. H." was a leading and prominent example. What she recommended to others she practised most thoroughly herself. The Bible was to her a mine of inexhaustible wealth; and from day to day she brought forth from it the hid treasures which enriched herself, and helped her to enrich others.

The memory of a visit paid to the home of the writer in 1877, is intimately associated with this marked feature of " F. R. H.'s " religious life. The younger members of our family, as well as our servants, were influenced by her winning and cheerful spirit, and the original and thoughtful comments she made on striking verses in the daily portions of Scripture read, excited great attention and interest. On Sunday morning especially, our Friend made it a point that each one at the breakfast-table should select a text from the BIBLE UNION Chapter; and the bright and happy remarks, and the variety of texts elicited, made even the youngest anticipate the pleasant exercise.

After she had left us, all were anxious to know the particular text of her weekly selection; and a request was made that the reference might be sent regularly on a post-card. The request was more than granted. The post-card was generally filled with references, and leading thoughts were worked out, evidently with much prayerful study.

---

[1] Information respecting this Union can be obtained from the Rev. Ernest Boys, M.A., Bengeo, Co. Hereford, England.

Early in the year 1879, our Friend visited us again. The post-cards had been carefully preserved in a suitable book, and she was not a little interested to find how numerous they were. A suggestion was then made, that what had been so profitable to ourselves might prove profitable to others, if the contents of the cards could be printed in a small volume. After some hesitation, on the ground of the notes not being designed for the public eye, "F. R. H." consented, and promised to revise them as soon as an opportunity could be found.

The opportunity never came: the Sweet Singer's Home Call was near at hand. The last post-card with the selected text, "This thing is from Me" (*1 Kings* 12:24), reached us shortly before she "fell asleep"; and in the sadness of heart which prompted us to ask "Why one so fitted for the Master's service should be taken?" the week's message from the Word seemed to bring us the Divine Answer, "What I do, thou knowest not now, but thou shalt know hereafter."

The notes on the post-cards have been reproduced in facsimile, in order to retain as far as possible their fresh and original attractiveness. With the exception of the omission of a few words of a personal character on several cards, no alteration has been made; but since the notes on some were very brief, it has been thought best to select those which were the most complete, and to arrange them for the Sundays of a Year. The reader will feel that each card is well termed "A BIBLE STUDY," and the writing out of the references will, I trust, furnish, in many homes, material for deeply interesting Sunday morning exercises.

As the most fitting introduction of these memorials of one of whom it may so truly be said that "being dead she yet speaketh," I would commend the following passage from "ROYAL COMMANDMENTS," in which the study of THE WORD is urged with loving earnestness, as the means whereby we may most surely hope, by the Divine Spirit's teaching, to "grow in grace, and in the knowledge of our Lord and Saviour Jesus Christ."

"He hath said, 'Search the Scriptures; for ... they are they which testify of Me.' Are we really searching, or only superficially reading, those Old Testament Scriptures of which He spoke? He says they testify of Him, *i.e.,* tell us all about Him; are we acting as if we quite believed that?

"'Beginning at Moses and all the Prophets, He expounded unto them in ALL the Scriptures, the things concerning Himself.' Then there are things about Jesus in ALL the Scriptures—not just only in the Psalms and Isaiah, but in every book! How very much there must be for us to find! Let us ask the Holy Spirit to take of these 'things of Jesus' and 'show them unto us,' that we may grow in 'the knowledge of the Son of God.'

"The words which I speak unto you, they are spirit and they are life!"—quickening and continually life-giving words. We want to be permeated with them;

we want them to dwell in us richly: to be the inspiration of our whole lives, the very music of our spirits, whose melodious overflow may be glory to God, and good-will to man.

> *"Let me then be always growing,*
> *Never, never standing still:*
> *Listening, learning, better knowing*
> *Thee, and Thy most blessed will:*
> *That the Master's eye may trace,*
> *Day by day, my growth in grace."*

F. R. H.

H.B.[1]

7 The Paragon, Blackheath, S.E.
August, 1880.

[1] "H.B." was Mrs. Charles Bullock.

From a Photograph by F. C. Earl, *Worcester.*   *Engraved by* R. & E. Taylor.

ASTLEY CHURCH, THE RECTORY, AND CHURCHYARD.

The Early Home and Resting Place of F. R. H.   The Tomb is beneath the spreading fir tree.

This print and the "Mumbles' Lighthouse" were the only illustrations in the original book, My Bible Study: *for the Sundays of the Year.*

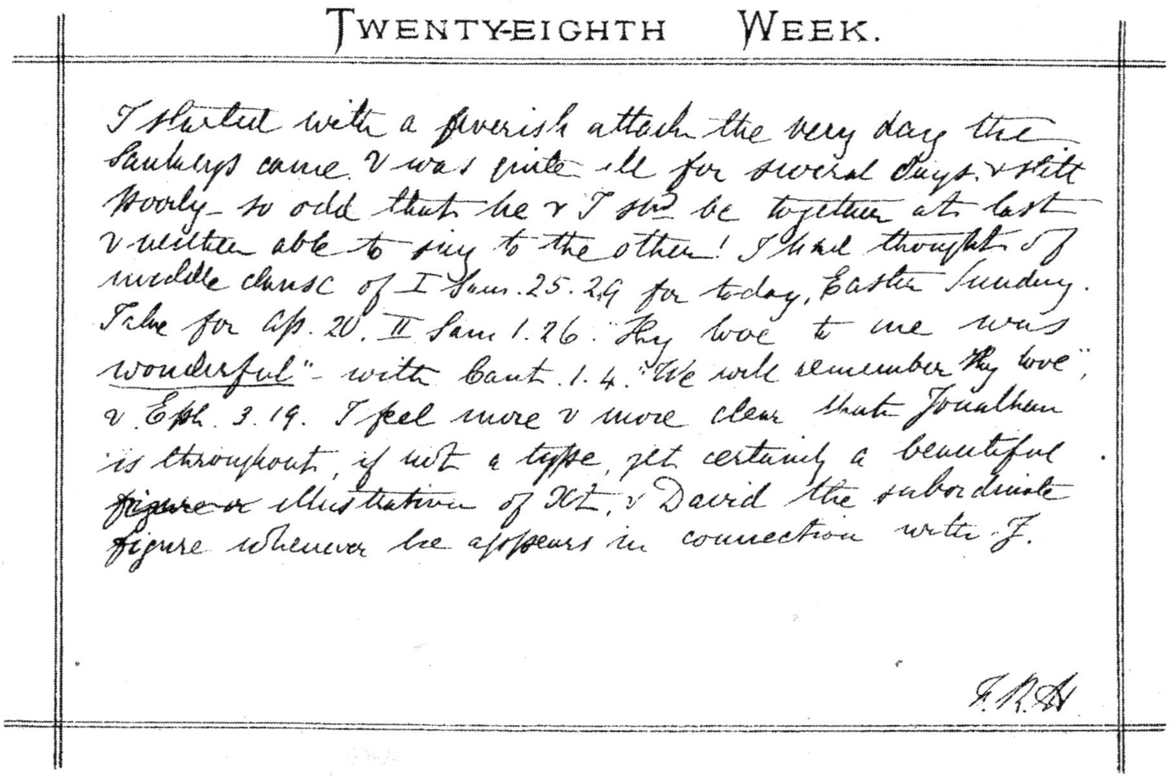
TWENTY-EIGHTH WEEK.

I started with a feverish attack the very day the
Sankeys came & was quite ill for several days, & still
poorly — so odd that he & I shd be together at last
& neither able to sing to the other! I had thought of
middle clause of I Sam. 25. 29 for to-day, Easter Sunday.
Take for Ap. 20. II Sam. 1.26. "thy love to me was
wonderful" — with Cant. 1. 4. "We will remember thy love",
& Eph. 3. 19. I feel more & more clear that Jonathan
is throughout, if not a type, yet certainly a beautiful
~~figure or~~ illustration of Xt, & David the subordinate
figure whenever he appears in connection with J.

F.R.H.

This was written very late in her life. Ira Sankey, the music leader under Dwight L. Moody, visited Frances, likely either after Easter or in May, before she died June 3, 1879. Rev. Bullock published My Bible Study: for the Sundays of the Year *in regular typeset text, a small book, and also in a larger facsimile edition, giving facsimile reprints of the 52 original cards in F.R.H.'s handwriting. This was the Twenty-eighth Week, on page 49.*

My Bible Study

Thy Word.

Upon Thy Word I rest,
So strong, so sure:
So full of comfort blest,
So sweet, so pure.
The Word that changeth not, that faileth never!
My King, I rest upon Thy Word for ever!

F. R. H.

FIRST WEEK.

For October 7. I have just been reading Ecclesiastes 5, and am most struck with "Defer not to pay it," in connection with "Take my life," etc. Then the *grand* title—"He that is higher than the highest," rfs. Isaiah 57:15, and Revelation 19:16. And lastly, the thought of God's giving "power to rejoice in his labour; *this* is the gift of God." How all our work might have been *in itself* distressing and painful! It seems a new subject of thanksgiving, so good of Him to value us *like* the work He assigns us. I glanced on to to-morrow's chap., and greatly like "Who knoweth what is good for man in this life," with Psalm 47:4, and 85:12.

F. R. H.

SECOND WEEK.

For Sunday, October 13. Exodus 29:33—"And they shall eat those things whereof the atonement was made." Does not this point to John 6:53–55? The continual feeding in our heart by faith with thanksgiving—really *living on* "those things"—*i.e.*, Christ Himself and His precious blood. "Eat" is so much more than just knowing about them; it implies personal and active appropriation, and also sense of need, and then finding satisfaction. Does the plural "things" imply all the components, so to speak, of the one great atonement? If so, we must go back to the Father's love and purpose and provision (Genesis 22:8), and Christ's love and willingness to do His Father's will—and then "Thy Cross and Passion, Thy precious death"—the sacred body offered, the precious blood shed. Now, may you and I, dear H., "eat" those things not only next Sunday, but every day, and be consecrated and sanctified by them.

THIRD WEEK.

For October 20. Exodus 36:7. God's supply of materials to His workers by human wills. When Bezaleel and Aholiab got the "pattern" they might have wondered where all the "stuff" was to come from. There was no command, no cloy, but hearts were touched by God (1 Chronicles 29:14). If any work is really God's giving, and He puts it into our hearts either to "devise" (Exodus 35:32),

and into the power of our hands to "do," (v. 35) no fear but He will also provide "stuff" sufficient, whether metal or mental!

FOURTH WEEK.

FOR October 27. Leviticus 3:2, first clause. Personal interest in the peace-
offering. "For He is our Peace." "My faith would lay her hand, etc." "For He
hath made Him to be sin for us who knew no sin, that we might be made the
righteousness of God in Him." Therefore, being justified by faith, (*i.e.* laying
the hand on the head of our peace-offering), we have peace with God through
our Lord Jesus Christ. Touching sin conveys sin, touching the sinless one conveys purity. For peace *and* purity flow from Him.

FIFTH WEEK.

FOR November 3. Leviticus 10:7. "The anointing oil of the Lord is upon
you." *For* He "hath made us kings and priests," Revelation 1:6. And "their
anointing shall be, etc., etc., everlasting," Exodus 40:15, "holy," and "royal,"
1 Peter 2:5, 9. "Is upon *you,*" 1 John 2:20, because upon *Him,* John 3:34, and
Psalm 133:2. It is also "oil of joy," Isaiah 61:3. Compare Psalm 45:7 with John
15:11, "My joy." Compare Exodus 29:21—no anointing with oil without first
sprinkling with blood—compare with this Revelation 1:5, 6, "blood" and *then*
"kings and priests." See Psalm 105:15, protection of anointed ones.
Past—2 Corinthians 1:21.
Present—Psalm 23:5.
Future—Psalm 92:10.

SIXTH WEEK.

FOR Sunday, November 10. Leviticus 17:11. I suppose this is the verse
Dr. A. means in his "Notes" in C.P. as being the key to the whole book.
Wonder how Farrar & Co. get over it, especially as confirmed with Hebrews
9:22! I am especially struck with "I have given it you upon the altar," the
very blood of Christ being Jehovah's *gifts* "given *upon the altar,*" with all its
connected thoughts of slaying, suffering, and consuming by fire. For *thus* was
His precious blood "given to you." What do we receive by this gift of blood?
1. Atonement, Leviticus 17:11. 2. Redemption, Ephesians 1:7; 1 Peter 1:19,
20; Revelation 1:5. 3. Remission of sins, Matthew 26:28; Romans 3:25;

Hebrews 9:22. 4. Peace, Colossians 1:20. 5. Justification, Romans 5:9. 6. Cleansing, 1 John 1:7; Revelation 1:5. 7. Nearness to God, Ephesians 2:13. 8. Access into the Holiest, Hebrews 10:19. And 10. Everlasting life, John 6:54. Really it is everything!

[Note: In the original hand-written post-card for the Sixth Week, F. R. H. went from number 8 to number 10.   D.C., June 2004]

SEVENTH WEEK.

For Sunday, November 17. Leviticus 24:2. "Pure oil olive *to cause the lamps to burn continually.*" Connect Philippians 1:19. "The *supply* of the Spirit of Jesus Christ," and 2:15, "ye shine, etc." Take the two "*lets*"—Matthew 5:16, and Luke 12:35. See Matthew 24:4 and verse 9, "*buy for yourselves,*" (which that clever cleric objected to) "without money and without price," for Luke 11:13. Connect this command with the "*Command*" in our verse—not a mere permission. There is no shining with borrowed oil. But there shall be oil for oil, see 2 Kings 4:2 and 6—so "grace for grace."

EIGHTH WEEK.

For Sunday, November 24. Numbers 4:19, last half. Compare 2 Chronicles 2:18, Solomon (type of Christ) doing same as Aaron here. *Every one.* 1. "Work," Mark 13:34. 2. "According to *ability,*" Matthew 25:15. 3. "Over against his own *house,*" Nehemiah 3:28. 4. "Reward," 1 Corinthians 3:8. See 1 Thessalonians 4:11, "our business," but that should be 1 Chronicles 26:30. "*Appoints.*" Ephesians 2:10—see margin.
  "Service *and* burden"—illustrated by Acts 9:6 and 16—"do" and "suffer." General reference—1 Corinthians 12:18, but read on to verse 22. And finish with Revelation 2:10.

"Open Thou mine eyes to see
All the work Thou hast for me."

"The time, the place, the way
He knows it all;
Do well thy work to-day,
And wait His call."—*Anon.*

NINTH WEEK.

For Sunday, December 1. Numbers 11:23. *Question—Father.* "Is the Lord's (Jehovah's) hand, etc." *Son.* Isaiah 50:2. Spirit, Micah 2:7. *Answer,* Isaiah 59:1. *Question*—Genesis 18:14 and Jeremiah 32:27. *Answer,* Jeremiah 32:17 and Job 42:2. Negative, Luke 1:37. Positive, Matthew 19:26. "Thou shalt *see* now, etc." Numbers 23:19; Isaiah 14:27. *Judicial* instances, 2 Kings 7:2; Isaiah 26:11; Jeremiah 44:28, 29. *Gracious* instances, Genesis 48:11; Luke 2:30. Not forgetting that Dec. 1 is Advent Sunday, connects this "shalt, etc.," with Isaiah 33:17, and Revelation 1:7. For *this* "word shall come to pass."

TENTH WEEK.

For December 8. Numbers 18:7. "I have given your priest's office unto you *as a service of gift.*" Did you ever reckon *this* among the Father's "good gifts"? the "holy" and "royal" and "everlasting" priesthood "given to Christ" *and* to the "many sons" whom He is bringing unto glory?

ELEVENTH WEEK.

For Sunday, December 15. Numbers 25:11. "Zealous *for my sake*"—the dividing line between right and wrong zeal, the test of motive. Zeal itself *an attribute of God,* see margin "with my zeal," 2 Kings 19:31; Isaiah 63:15; Ezekiel 5:13. *Christ the example of zeal,* Isaiah 59:17; compare zeal of the Father for the Son, Isaiah 9:7, and zeal of the Son for the Father, Psalm 69:9, and John 2:17. Examples of holy zeal; David, Psalm 119:139; the Corinthians, 2 Corinthians 9:2; Epaphras, Colossians 4:13. See Galatians 4:18; explained by Titus 2:14— z. of *good works,* and 1 Corinthians 14:12,—z. of *sp. gifts.* Compare Revelation 3:19, with 2 Corinthians 7:11—repentance and zeal together.

Wrong kinds—Ostentatious z., 2 Kings 10:16. Partisan zeal, Galatians 4:17. Ignorant z., Romans 10:2, and Acts 22:3. Persecuting z., 2 Samuel 21:2; Philippians 3:6. Mistaken z., Acts 21:20; Galatians 1:14. And I think that's all there is about it. Oh that all our zeal may be "for *thy* sake"—"for Jesus' sake only."

TWELFTH WEEK

For Sunday, December 22. Numbers 32:6 and 23. The sin that shall find us out is one of omission, simply *not* going to war, but sitting still. The sin of Sodom was just idleness and *not* doing active good, see Ezekiel 16:49. Compare "*not*" in Nehemiah 3:5, and Judges 5:23. Not going to war with our brethren is sinning "against the Lord," Numbers 32:23, for it is not going with *Him*—compare 2 Samuel 19:25, and Luke 11:23. See Hebrews 6:12, and 2 Timothy 2:3. For *our King* says: "Be thou valiant for me, and fight the Lord's battles," 1 Samuel 18:17.

THIRTEENTH WEEK.

For Sunday, December 29, 1878. Deuteronomy 3:24. "O Lord God, thou hast *begun to shew* thy servant thy greatness." We can't conceive God doing anything incompletely, 1 Samuel 3:12, (last part) so *beginning* to shew implies a pledge. John 1:50; Jeremiah 33:3, and supplies a plea, Micah 7:15. All God's revealings are only "*beginning* to shew," Job 26:14. Was there a progressive "showing" even to the Son in his human nature? John 5:20. I wonder if Moses thought of his prayer in Exodus 33:18, and if he thought of that *with* the present verse in his own Psalm 90 verse 16, *P. B. V.* Compare Deuteronomy 2:31, "begun to give," and *therefore* "begin to possess." Is there not a corresponding "therefore" to follow "begun to show"?

FOURTEENTH WEEK.

For Sunday, January 5. Deuteronomy 10:21. *Response found in*: He is thy praise, Jeremiah 17:14; He is thy God, Psalm 63:1; He is thy life, Deuteronomy 30:20; Psalm 27:1; He is thy Lord, Psalm 45:11; Psalm 16:2.

FIFTEENTH WEEK.

For Sunday, January 12. Deuteronomy 17:15. The *right* king should be: 1*st, Chosen of God.* So Christ is—1 Peter 2:4; Psalm 89:19; Isaiah 42:1. *2nd, One from among thy brethren, e.g.,* 2 Samuel 19:12, 42. See Jeremiah 30:21, "their governor." Christ is our King, and yet "thy brother"; "not a stranger," see Job 19:27, margin. Same as "priest," Exodus 28:1, ("thy brother"); and "prophet." Deuteronomy 18:15, 18. It seems to me that we get this threefold thought as to the brotherhood of Christ in Hebrews 2; in *v.* 12, "declaring" as *Prophet* to His brethren, *v.* 14, overcoming and destroying as *King* while taking part of our flesh and blood, and *v.* 17, made like unto His brethren that He might be a merciful and faithful High *Priest.* Because *we* are "chosen *in* Him," we are "a chosen generation, a *royal priesthood,*" to "*shew forth,*" etc., *(prophethood).*

Thanks for *charming* journal,[1] Jan. 6.

---

[1] This refers to a little book entitled "Journal of Mercies," arranged by Mrs. Sandberg.

SIXTEENTH WEEK.

FOR Sunday, January 19. Deuteronomy 24:18. "*Remember*"—a holy word of Deuteronomy—generally followed by a practical "therefore." See also c. 5:15; 8:2, 6; 15:15. Remember, 1*st,* "that bondman"—command *five times* repeated. See Isaiah 51:1, and Deuteronomy 9:7. Compare Lamentations 3:20. Contrast Hebrews 8:12, and Isaiah 43:25. 2nd, that ... redeemed thee. From *nine* things—see what. (1). Deuteronomy 13:5; (2). Psalm 103:4; (3). Hosea 13:14; (4). Galatians 3:13; (5). Deuteronomy 7:8, and Psalm 106:10; (6). Psalm 136:24; (7). Genesis 48:16; (8). 1 Peter 1:18; (9). Titus 2:14. We shall "remember" this forever. Revelation 5:9. Note Deuteronomy 16:3, "remember the *day.*" Our verse, with verse 18 and c. 15:15, and contexts seem to make kindness to the poor almost a sacramental act—"do this thing" in remembrance of thy redemption—with Luke 22:19.

SEVENTEENTH WEEK.

FOR Sunday, January 26. Deuteronomy 31:6. "The Lord thy God, He it is that doth go *with* thee." In verse 8 we have "before"; in Isaiah 52:12, "rereward." Thus the Lord *thy* God, ("God, even our *own* God") *compasses* us, Psalm 139:3, and Deuteronomy 32:10, margin. See "*behind* and *before.*" Psalm 139:5. Same thoughts as to Jehovah Jesus, Matthew 28:20 "with"; John 10:4, "before"; Luke 10:1, last clause implying the "behind." I can't think of any parallels to carry it out as to the Holy Spirit, perhaps there are some.

I have *taken* to your "Journal,"[1] and like it greatly. I put down which-ever "mercy" seems *uppermost* in my mind for each day, *not one in a thousand, though!*

[1] "Journal of Mercies." (See Fifteenth Week.)

EIGHTEENTH WEEK.

For Sunday, February 2, 1879. Joshua 4:14; 1*st* part, typically considered. "*On that day*" holds good in either interpretation, either as passing over into the land of spiritual promise, or into the heavenly Canaan. "On that day" Jesus is "magnified" in the sight of His people. Connect Philippians 1:20. Compare two royal types (or illustrations), 1 Chronicles 29:25, and 2 Chronicles 32:23. In the first the magnification results from will. My submission and joyful coronation (verses 22–24); in the 2nd, from the bringing of presents (see margin) to the king; thus both point to Christ being magnified *in our* life by consecration of ourselves and our service.

NINETEENTH WEEK.

For February 9. Joshua 11:15. "*He* left nothing undone of all that the Lord commanded Moses." "*We* have left undone those things which we ought to have done." But Romans 10:4. "For He says I came not," etc., Matthew 5:17; Hebrews 10:7, God's "will" being expressed in His law. Isaiah 42:21; Romans 5:19.

TWENTIETH WEEK.

On Sunday I dwelt on six special bits in Obadiah. I will simply give you them as marked in my Bible:

v. 3. The pride of thine heart hath deceived thee.

v. 6. How are his hidden things revealed. 1 Corinthians 4:5; Matthew 10:26; and a railway down to Jonah 1:7, last clause.

v. 11. Thou stoodest on the other side. Luke 10:32.

v. 15. As thou hast done, it shall be done unto thee. Matthew 7:2.

v. 17. *There* shall be holiness. Zechariah 14:210, 21; Isaiah 35:8, and Revelation 21:27.

v. 21. The kingdom shall be the Lord's. I think I dwelt about equally on each, every one seemed so full of teaching, though I did not do much referencing. I have not yet looked at Micah 3 for the 23d.

TWENTY-FIRST WEEK.

FOR Sunday, February 23. Judges 1:3. Compare Hebrews 10:24. We have each our separate "*lot*" to conquer, but here is a mint of help, which we shall find real. The usual thing is to help or expect to be helped by other folks in this war of extermination and possession, but you see Judah did not even go so far as his half-brother; it was Simeon, his *own* brother, to whom he went. Satan is quick enough to know how much brothers and sisters and very near relatives generally *might* help each other, and I think that quite accounts for the difficulty so very often felt in breaking the ice! Singular, too, that the wish and requests for help came not from the smaller, but the larger tribe, and from one of the great standard-bearers. Is there a type here of the Lion of the tribe of Judah condescending to ask and accept helpers? See Judges 5:23. Jesus calling His weak brethren to fight in His great battles, and then promising to fight ours! "I likewise will go with thee into thy lot." Though "Simeon went with him," there is no mention of his help, the victories were all Judah's triumph when he "went with Simeon his brother" (vs. 17, 18).

TWENTY-SECOND WEEK.

FOR Sunday, March 2. Judges 8:1. A lesson on *touchiness.* Pride is always at the bottom of it; envy and want of love come next in it, and exaggeration and anger often grow out of it. It is not an infirmity, but *a great sin.* Galatians 5:26; 1 Corinthians 13:4, 5. Christ's true soldiers should be willing and nowhere in the way if so He orders. Jeremiah 45:5, first part. Study Ephraim's touchiness. See *unreasonableness.* Gideon had called those tribes nearest scene of action, *cf.* ch. 6:33, 35. See *exaggeration; cf.*, Gideon *had* called them to a special service, ch. 7:24. See egotism, "callest *us* not!" *compare very carefully* the details of ch. 12:1, 2, and see how sin indulged grows and develops—same fault, but now in *action* as well as word (c. 8:1, "said"; c. 12:1, "gathered"). Exaggeration grown to falsehood, having *been* called and refused "to come"; anger grown into horrible threats and revenge, ("chide sharply," grown to "we will *burn,* etc.") When the iniquity is full the punishment falls, ch. 12. verses 4–6; brought on themselves by their own touchiness! Great lesson, Philippians 2:3–5.

TWENTY-THIRD WEEK.

For March 9. Judges 15:18. Not a model prayer as to tone and spirit,[1] for there is a sound of petulance and unbelief in it, but excellent in its argument, basing what we would have God do on what He has already done. Compare Psalm 56:13; Psalm 3:7; Psalm 61:2, 3; Judges 1:15; Romans 8:32; 2 Corinthians 1:10. When the Lord has delivered our soul (Psalm 55:18, and Psalm 56:13), "from the battle" and "from death," we may be very sure He will not suffer it either to famish (Proverbs 10:3), or to thirst (John 4:14), nor to fall into the hand of the enemy, (Luke 1:71, 74; Psalm 37:33).

[1] Contrast Samson's mother's *tone* in ch. 13:23.

TWENTY-FOURTH WEEK.

For March 16, 1879. Ruth 1:18. "*When* she saw, etc., *then* she left, etc." The advantage of *decision* for Christ. Steadfast purpose escapes a vast deal of temptation. People *see* it is no use! Instances: Rebekah, Genesis 24:58, 59; Daniel, Daniel 1:8, 16; St. Paul, Acts 21:14. A *remarkable* one in 1 Kings 1:8 and 26. Those who did not let Adonijah tamper with them were "not called" to join in his treason. See St. Paul's "purpose" in 2 Timothy 3:10, an illustration of it in 1 Corinthians 2. When one really says with full *purpose,* "One thing I do," one escapes a whole set of temptations as a matter of course. Just fancy anyone inviting * * * * to a ball or * * * * to a theatre! and it's just the same with *any* really "on the Lord's side," no matter how young. They wouldn't ask * * * * for instance. And the principle extends much farther. Let us consider Acts 11:23.

TWENTY-FIFTH WEEK.

For March 23, 1879. 1 Samuel 3:18, last clause. "*Let* Him do, etc." A *very* favourite word of mine. When we "*let* Him do" it, we prove what is that "good," etc., etc., see Romans 12:2. Eli said, "*let*" in submissive *certainty* that terrible things were coming, because foretold. But we sometimes hesitate to say "Let" when there is no such certainty. Throw the accent on the next word, and say, "Let *Him*," and then the "let" comes easy. In each instance of this submission in *un*certainty, deliverance and blessing followed. See the type of Gibeon and Joshua, Joshua 9:25, 26 and 10:6–14; then see Judges 10:15, 16 and 11:32, 33; then 2 Samuel 10:12, 13; then 2 Samuel 15:26 and 19:14 and 22:1. "Secureth *good*" (Heb., good in His eyes), what *He* calls *good* must be *best*, generally a good deal better than our best. See Jeremiah 18:4, that clay vessel could not guess how good it was going to be made. Let us *always* say, Matthew 11:26.

TWENTY-SIXTH WEEK.

I forgot to put down your address. Also I found I counted the chapters wrong, and ought to have given you a text from the *Fourth*. Then I *intended* to have given you 1 Samuel 10:19, "*rejected* of God who *Himself* saved you"—with Isaiah 53:3; but now see the *Eleventh* is the chapter. So I send for March 30, 1 Samuel 11:9. A Royal message and the result of its reception. *Promised help* for the day of need (Psalm 50:15); *simple belief* that the King would be as good as His word, able and willing to deliver when no other could (see 1 Samuel 11:3); and *consequent gladness*. See the margin, "God's *help*" is also "deliverance," and both are included in "Salvation," (make a railway to verse 13). "Let us therefore," etc. Hebrews 4:16; Psalm 70:5. Connect Luke 2:10, and Romans 10:15. What higher ambition or joy can we have than to be "messengers of the King's" help? Interesting to compare 1 Samuel 31:11, 13, showing grateful remembrance.

TWENTY-SEVENTH WEEK.

For Sunday, April 6. 1 Samuel 18:4. I don't know if I am right, but it seems to me that in the friendship with Jonathan David's typical character as "king" is left out of sight, and he here illustrates our relationship to the King's *Son*. Then this verse is an exquisite picture, Christ *stripping* Himself, Philippians 2:7, and John 13:4; "*the robe that* was *upon Him*," John 17:22; "*gave it to D.*" Isaiah 61:10, Ezekiel 16:8, (*my* skirts) "Sword" connects Ephesians 6:17 with "*given*" in John 17:14. "*Bow.*" See Job 29:20, margin "*changed*," just our weak bow changed for His strong one. Genesis 49:24, "*Girdle*," Isaiah 11:5, 1 Corinthians 1:30; Revelation 17:14 (*faithful*). *Why* all this? "*Because* he loved him."

TWENTY-EIGHTH WEEK.

I STARTED with a feverish attack the very day the Sankeys came, and was quite ill for several days, and still poorly—so odd that he and I should be together at last, and neither able to sing to the other! I had thought of middle clause of 1 Samuel 25:2, 9, for to-day, Easter Sunday. Take for April 20, 2 Samuel 1:26, "Thy love to me was *wonderful*," with Song of Solomon 1:4, "We will remember Thy love," and Ephesians 3:19. I feel more and more clear that Jonathan is throughout, if not a type, yet certainly a beautiful illustration of Christ, and David the subordinate figure whenever he appears in connection with J.

TWENTY-NINTH WEEK.

FOR April 27. 2 Samuel 8:18, last bit. "David's sons were chief rulers"; margin "*princes.*" That is the dignity of the adopted children of the King—see 1 Samuel 11:8; Psalm 113:8. Observe particularly *Psalm* 45:16, *Thy children* "whom Thou mayest make *princes.*" Then see Jeremiah 17:25, and compare with Revelation 1:6, and Job 36:7. Thus Christ is the Prince of princes, Daniel 8:25, in a spiritual sense, and see that touching verse, Hosea 8:10. If *princes*, let us claim and use the power of a prince, see Genesis 32:28, and Hosea 12:3, margin. "*Knowing the weight* of thy royal degree," says Miss Elliott. I'm going to send these texts, with 2 Samuel 20:26 (*margin*), to "Ira" D. Sankey!

THIRTIETH WEEK.

FOR Sunday, May 4. 2 Samuel 15:22, last bit. All the little ones that were with him, and with Matthew 18:6, "these little ones who believe on Me!"

For May 11, we have an "embarras de re chesses" indeed! I take 2 Samuel 7 in v. 28, "Thy words be true!" That's enough.

THIRTY-FIRST WEEK.

I CHOOSE for next Sunday (May 18) 1 Kings 5:17. "*The King*" "*commanded*" "*great* stones,"—"*costly* stones," "*hewed* stones," "foundation of the house." Those six points will bear a lot of referencing. The point that struck me being all these great, costly, and hewed stones, being laid *out of sight,* yet making the strong, needed foundation for a beautiful superstructure. Do you see my thought?

THIRTY-SECOND WEEK.

For May 25. 1 King 12:24. "*This* thing is from Me"—(railway to v. 15). If anything *wasn't* from the Lord, one would have thought His infatuation was that thing! So it seems a lesson of acquiescence in those *most* difficult things to acquiesce in,—*i.e.*, what seems to arise from man's (or *lads'*!) foolishness and tryingness. See 2 Corinthians 5:18, "*all* things"*;* and 2 Corinthians 4:15. Compare Genesis 45:8 and 50:20.

Note.—The Post Card dated May 25 (1879), was the last received. On June 3d, the King's message reached our dear Friend. How truly, as she entered within the Palace Gates, did she recognize His loving voice, "*This* thing is from *Me!*"

The added Post Cards are selected from those received during 1877 and 1878. Some cards were lost, and others were briefly written during this period; so that the arrangement of dates is necessarily irregular. — H.B.

THIRTY-THIRD WEEK.

Isaiah 42:11. Let the inhabitants of the rock sing. Psalm 18:2,—"*is my* Rock."

Three steps, Psalm 61:2, "lead—to"; 40:2, "set feet upon"; 27:5, "set me *up* upon."

See Exodus 33:21,—"shalt stand upon," and yet next verse, "put thee in clift of." Place for the feeblest.—Proverbs 30:26; then Psalm 91:1. Use the appeal to spiritual Moabites—Jeremiah 48:28. Is not dwelling synonymous with continually trusting? See Isaiah 26:4, *margin.* If so, Psalm 5:11, Let all those that put their trust in Thee rejoice, is the *literal* form of this figurative text.

Isaiah 12 seems the song of the inhab. of the Rock.

THIRTY-FOURTH WEEK.

For April 14. Ezekiel 24:25. "When I take from them ... that whereupon they *set their minds.*" How often we hear that expression. Contrast Colossians 3:2, margin, and Luke 10:42. See Psalm 91:14, "set his *love* upon *Me,*" and Isaiah 26:3, "*mind* is stayed on Thee." Then Ezekiel 40:4, "set thy heart on all that *I* shall shew thee." Illustration, Proverbs 24:32, margin. See 1 Chronicles 29:3, "set my affection."

THIRTY-FIFTH WEEK.

EZEKIEL 45:4. "Which shall come near to minister unto the Lord." No ministering without coming near, 40:46; 43:19; 44:15, 16. We are—1. *Chosen* to come near, Numbers 16:5; 2. *Called* to come near, 2 Chronicles 29:31; 3. *Caused* to come near, Jeremiah 30:21. Then "Blessed is ... whom Thou choosest and causest," etc., etc., Psalm 65:4.

How we come near, Ephesians 2:14; Hebrews 10:19–22; then Hebrews 13:15, 16.

THIRTY-SIXTH WEEK.

FOR Sunday, May 19. Daniel 11:35. And some of them of understanding shall fall *to try by them* (margin). Certainly this is being fulfilled nowadays— these *very* clever intellectual men falling into various degrees of error. Is it not that God will "try by them" who is content to take His "word only," and who is not "rooted and built up," but swayed hither and thither by man's words and influence? It seems to me that Jeremiah 17:5 has special force when applied to this intellectually trusting in man, also Isaiah 2:22 to the way in which so many are tempted to take man's word, especially if a favourite scientific or religious leader or periodical, instead of *God's* utterances.

THIRTY-SEVENTH WEEK.

FOR May 26. Hosea 5:13. "Yet could he *not* heal." Mark 5:26; Job 13:4; Psalm 108:12, with Hosea 6:1. "*He will heal us.*" Compare ch. 11:3, "KNEW NOT." See Jeremiah 30:12–17, notice "for" in verse 14. *Exodus* 15:26; Deuteronomy 32:39; *Isaiah 53:5, and Psalm 30:2.* Jeremiah 17:14, "*shall*," Jeremiah 33:6, 2 Chronicles 30:20, Malachi 4:2. I never shall forget a friend of mine reading Isaiah 53, and stopping short in verse 5,—"And with His stripes we are ... *made a little better?*" Oh for more practical faith in the *Healer* of souls! How few expect Him to do more than "make them a little better" in the teeth of "He *will* heal" and all the other promises.

THIRTY-EIGHTH WEEK.

For June 2. Hosea 13:9. "In Me *is* thine help," not merely "I will help thee," Psalm 89:19. Then I was thinking of looking out all the other things which we have "*in* Him," *e.g.,* Isaiah 45:24; Ephesians 1:7, 11; John 16:33, etc.; but not time to work them out this morning.

THIRTY- NINTH WEEK.

For Sunday, June 9, 1878. Amos 3:7, with Psalm 25:14. But this is "*servants,*" and "I have called you *friends.*" I think this revealing is not at an end, and the closer walking there is with God the more there will be of it. It is an intensely interesting subject to me, though I almost never say anything about it. There seem intimations that He will shew His "friends" secrets, and don't we often get intimations which cannot be accounted for by mere coincidence? Presentiments which are His preparations leading to pray or *not* to pray for certain persons or things, and so on. We have not fathomed His "friendship" even in these directions. John 16:13; 15:15.

FORTIETH WEEK.

Friday. Micah 3:8, for June 23. New Testament parallel seems to be 2 Timothy 1:7. These are both *acknowledgments* of the gift, Philemon 6. This "full of power" only "by the Spirit of the Lord"—see Acts 6:3, 5, 8.—Four things Stephen was full of. Jesus says "Thine (Father) is the power";—then, "All power is given unto Me"; and "All things that the Father hath are Mine." Then "All are *yours*"—"power" included—ours *from* the Father, in Christ, *through* the Spirit. See Luke 10:19. "Behold, I give unto you power ... over all the power of the enemy." But the special power in Micah 3:8, is power by the Spirit to be instrumental in one great work of the Spirit "convincing of sin," (John 16:8); "to declare unto Israel," etc., etc.

Don't we want just *this* power?

In how many cases we (at any rate I can speak for myself) have failed to reach a heart by even the most fervent telling of the love of Jesus, *because* we have not been full of power to declare unto "Jacob his *sin!*" Until this is "declared," whether by human instrumentality or by the voice of the Spirit *alone;* all we can say of Jesus is only as "a very lowly song."

It was the son of thunder who was also the apostle of love. I'm writing out on the rocks, and the waves are coming in grandly, so I have been writing rather distractedly; but you'll get more than I out of the verse, so I'll give up and look at the waves.

FORTY-FIRST WEEK.

For Sunday, June 30. Nahum 3:11. "*Thou shalt be hid.*" Connect with ch. 1:14. "I will make thy grave." Remarkably fulfilled to the letter. Nineveh being "hid" and *buried* for 2,400 years. Literal fulfilment of these words, as *threat* argues fulfilment of the *very same words as* promise, Job 5:21.

"Thou shalt be hid!"

From—

(1), the scourge of the tongue, Job 5:21.

(2), the wicked, Psalm 17:9.

(3), the secret counsel of the wicked, Psalm 64:2.

Under—

the shadow of Thy wings, Psalm 17:8.

In—

(1), His pavilion, Psalm 27:5.

(2), the secret of His presence, Psalm 31:20.

(3), the shadow of His hand, Isaiah 49:2.

(4), His quiver, Isaiah 49:2.

With—

Christ in God, Colossians 3:3.

When?—

In the time of trouble, Psalm 27:5.

In the day of the Lord's anger, Zephaniah 2:3.

For—

Thou art my Hiding-place, Psalm 119:114; Psalm 32:7.

Therefore—

I flee unto Thee to hide me, Psalm 143:9.

So—

we are — "Thy hidden ones," Psalm 83:3.

FORTY-SECOND WEEK.

For July 7. "Consider your ways." Haggai 1:5. Will bear a lot of working out as to our "*ways*"; but I am TOO PRESSED to-day, and shall be travelling and "interviewing" all to-morrow. Ask the juveniles to find out how many things God tells us to "consider"; there are twelve or fourteen I know, and they make a very interesting set—a good concordance study, but best to try and think first *without*.

FORTY-THIRD WEEK.

For Sunday, July 14. Zechariah 6:11. "Make crowns, and set them upon the head of Joshua the High Priest." Revelation 19:12, "many." Is it not our privilege to have something to do with preparing these crowns and the jewels in them? You see it is "make," not merely "take." Meanwhile "WE see Him" already (Hebrews 2:9), "crowned with glory and honour." Outsiders don't see it at all, and many of us don't "see," because we don't steadily "look." I suppose it is the coronation day of Jesus in our hearts when we "take" all that is most precious to us, typified by the silver and gold, and "make crowns" with it for Him in the double aspects of "High Priest," *i.e.*, Atoner and Mediator, and Joshua our *accepted* and *recognized* "teacher and commander." I find THIS, Alice, takes me *much* longer than I expected. I can't bear doing anything *not* as well as ever I can, and the theme is too beautiful and important not to put my whole strength and care to it. So I *cannot* get it done *before* middle of this month. *So* much to do here. At work from A.M. till *late* P.M., now.

FORTY-FOURTH WEEK.

LEAMINGTON, July, 27. For Sunday, 28th. Genesis 2:22. "And brought her unto the man." So God the Father brings the Bride to the Second Adam— the Church collectively and each individually; for "No man can come to Me except the Father draw him," John 6:44. So our "coming" is God's "bringing" to "the Man Christ Jesus." Notice margin in preceding clause, "builded," pointing beautifully to Ephesians 2:22. *Just* occurs to me how remarkable the first clause—it is that which was first "*taken from*" which is "brought," so we are "chosen *in* Him," Ephesians 1:4, *before* being drawn. See the verses in John 17, about our being *given* to Christ. Four steps: 1. Chosen; 2. Given; 3. Drawn; 4. Preserved. What fourfold security!

FORTY-FIFTH WEEK.

AUGUST 5. Forgot to send! but you would not wonder if you knew all. I chose "The bow shall be SEEN in the cloud." Genesis 9:14. So we'll LOOK! We only *see* what we *look* at. That's why "men see *not*," etc. Job 37:21. Am buckling to at the Almanack—hope to finish by 11th or 13th, and post it to you. Haste.

Yours,   F.

FORTY-SIXTH WEEK.

FOR August 11. Genesis 16:13. "Have I also here *looked* after Him that seeth me?" Question for self-examination "*Here*"—in the particular place or circumstance or moment where we stand. "Have *I also?*" for *He* not only *sees*, but *looks*. Guidance of the eye, Psalm 32:8, must be met by looking. Compare Hebrews 11:27. See Psalm 123:1, 2; Psalm 141:8. Oh for fulfilment of Zechariah 9:1! I think there is a very present fulfilment of Isaiah 45:22; *if* we "look" we are "saved" from each sin or temptation as it arises. If we don't "look," *of course,* we see the waves and wind instead of Jesus, and then, *of course,* we begin to sink. When depressed or "bothered" let us say, "Have I also *here* looked?" For this always comes of *not* looking, for when we *do* look our faces must be lightened, Psalm 34:5. Even a "potsherd" shines in the sun!

FORTY-SEVENTH WEEK.

PIDWELL COTTAGE, Ashcott, Bridgewater. For August 25. Genesis 30:27. "The Lord hath blessed me for Thy sake." May this be a type of our being blessed for Christ's sake! ch. 28:14. "In thee and in thy seed, etc." Ephesians 1:3, "in Christ." Parallel—Joseph, ch. 39:3. When one says, as in ch. 32:10, "I am not worthy of the least," etc. "I deserve nothing—none of all this," then one thinks, "But Jesus deserved it for me. I am blessed thus for His sake."

FORTY-EIGHTH WEEK.

FOR September 1. Genesis 37:13. "Come, and I will send thee unto them. And he said to him, Here am I." See 1 John 4:14, and Hebrews 10:7, John 6:38. Then let us echo the "Here am I"—Isaiah 6:8, Joshua 1:16.

Unto me, Psalm 101:2.
—— thee, Zechariah 9:9.
—— him, John 14:23.
—— us, Isaiah 9:6.
—— you, Acts 3:26.
—— them, Matthew 21:37.

FORTY-NINTH WEEK.

ISAIAH 7:9, last half. Contrast "shalt not" with 2 Chronicles 20:20, "shall." I suppose this applies to *every separate* thing that God invites us to believe, "establishing," in any truth, or *any* grace or joy depends upon believing His word. But starting from "I know whom I have believed," "believing, we rejoice," and "My heart is *fixed*." See Psalm 112:7, 8, where it hinges on "trusting." 1 Peter 5:10.

FIFTIETH WEEK.

FOR Sunday, September 8. Genesis 44:33. "*Instead* of the lad." Just that one word: "instead of me." The love, willingness, and urgency of Judah. "Bound that I might be free" I suppose ὑπερ, in Romans 5:6, 8, is *really* "instead"; it is translated so in Philemon 13, "that in thy stead, etc." I never noticed before that the *reason* of "instead" is in the past, see previous verse, "became surety." So we go further back than the death of Christ in our stead, and get a glimpse of the everlasting love which "became surety" for us when He was yet in the bosom of the Father. See Titus 1:2, eternal life promised *before the world began*— to whom? *We* were not there to receive the promise—Christ received it *for* us, and holds it for us.

FIFTY-FIRST WEEK.

LOOSELEIGH, Tamerton, Plymouth, Sept. 13. For Sunday, Sept. 15. Exodus 1:12, last half; Genesis 41:52. Illustration (or type?) of Acts 8:4; 4:3, 4, etc. Also it seems to bear analogy to the work of grace in the soul, and suggests Bunyan's beautiful story of the fire burning higher and higher, the more the man tried to quench it with water.

FIFTY-SECOND WEEK.

In Exodus 15, verse 13, was *given* me if ever one was, and has been *delicious food* all the week, every word so peculiarly full of power and beauty to me. "*Thou* in Thy mercy *hast led forth Thy people* which *Thou* hast redeemed. *Thou* hast guided them in Thy strength unto Thy holy habitation." I have only time to *glance* at Exodus 22, for Sunday, but what catches my eye is verse 20, " Unto the Lord only." It brings up the whole subject of "*only* for Jesus"—the sacrifices of praise, love, bodies (Romans 12:1), "selves," etc., all "unto the Lord *only.*"

F. R. H.

Chapters learnt by F.R.H.

Genesis. 1. Learnt in Hebrew
     Sept. 1856.
Isaiah. 1.   ditto. Aug. 1856
—— 4 Learnt March 1852.
—— 12. Learnt   1846.
—— 35 Learnt   1847.
—— 40 Learnt   1849
—— 53. Learnt   1846.
—— 55. Learnt   1846.
—— 63. Learnt   1852.

The Epistle to the Romans.
  Finished learning Dec. 1854
Relearnt. Nov. 1857.
Galatians, Finished learning
     Feby 6th 1858.

Epistle to the Hebrews
  Finished learning Oct. 24 1857

Epistle of James
  Finished learning Nov. 9. 1857.

1st Epistle of Peter
  Finished learning Nov. 25. 1857.

2nd Epistle of Peter
  Finished learning Dec. 5. 1857.

1st Epistle of St John
  Finished learning Dec. 22. 1857.

2nd Epistle of St John
  Learnt Dec. 24. 1857.

3rd Epistle of John
  Learnt Dec. 26. 1857.

Epistle of Jude
  Learnt Dec. 30. 1857.

Revelation, chapters 1—6
  Learnt July 1852

Many other chapters are
scored with dates, but as it
is not stated that they were
learnt they have not been
added to this list.

This list was found among Havergal manuscripts and papers, likely gathered and written by one of her three sisters. We also know from her sister Maria that F.R.H. memorized all the New Testament except the Book of Acts, all the Minor Prophets, Isaiah, and all the Psalms.

This is the "Fourth Day" of F.R.H.'s 31-day book *Royal Commandments*.

The Means of Growth.

"Grow in grace, and in the knowledge of our Lord and Saviour Jesus Christ."
—2 Peter 3:18.

THE very thing we are longing to do, and perhaps mourning over not doing, and perhaps praying every day that we may do, and seeming to get no answer! But when God has annexed a means to the fulfilment of a command, we cannot expect Him to enable us to fulfil that command if we are not using His means. In this case the means are wrapped in another command: "Desire the sincere milk of the word, *that ye may grow* thereby."

1 Peter 2:2

Real desire must prove itself by action; it is no use desiring the milk and not drinking it. "Wherefore criest thou unto Me? speak unto the children of Israel, that they *go forward.*" Let us to-day, and every day henceforth, "go forward," and use in faith and honest earnestness this His own great means of growth.

Exodus 14:15

By the word we shall "grow in grace." The beginning of grace in our souls was by the same; for it is written, "Of His own will begat He us with the word of truth"; "Being born again, ... by the word of God." At every step it is the same word which develops the spiritual life. The young man shall "cleanse his way" by it. The entrance of it giveth light and understanding. The result of hiding it in our hearts is, that we "might not sin against Thee"; and how often by His word has He "withheld thee from sinning against Me!" Again and again we have said, "Thy word hath quickened me." For it comes to us "not in word only, but in power and in the Holy Ghost, and in much assurance." It is "able to make thee wise unto salvation," and its intended effects of reproof, correction, instruction in righteousness, rise to

James 1:18
1 Peter 1:23

Psalm 119:9
Psalm 119:130
Psalm 119:11

Genesis 20:6
Psalm 119:50
1 Thess. 1:5
2 Timothy 3:15

2 Timothy 3:16

what would seem a climax of growth, "that the man of God may be perfect, throughly furnished unto *all* good works." And yet there is a still more glorious result of this "word of God, which effectually worketh also in you that *believe*"; for by "His divine power" "are given unto us exceeding great and precious promises, that *by these* ye might be partakers of the divine nature." This is indeed the climax, for what can rise beyond this most marvellous effect of this blessed means of growth in grace! Oh, to use it as He would have us use it, so that every day we "may grow thereby"!

By the word we shall also grow in the knowledge of Christ. The mere surface of this is obvious. For how do we come to know more of any one whom having not seen, we love? Is it not by reading and hearing what he has said and written and done? How *are* we to know more of Jesus Christ, if we are not taking the trouble to know more of His word?

He hath said, "Search the Scriptures; for ... they are they which testify of Me." Are we really searching, or only superficially reading, those Old Testament Scriptures of which He spoke? He says they testify of Him, *i.e.* tell us all about Him; are we acting as if we quite believed that?

"Beginning at Moses and all the prophets, He expounded unto them in ALL the Scriptures the things concerning Himself." Then there are things about Jesus in *all* the Scriptures—not just only in the Psalms and Isaiah, but in every book! How very much there must be for us to find! Let us ask the Holy Spirit to take of *these* things of Jesus and show them unto us, that we may grow in "the knowledge of the Son of God."

"The words which I speak unto you, they are spirit, and they are life"—quickening and continually lifegiving words. We want to be permeated with them; we want them to dwell in us richly, to be the inspiration of our whole lives, the very music of our spirits, whose melodious overflow may be glory to God and goodwill to man. Jesus Himself has given us this quick and powerful word of God, and our responsibility is tremendous. He has told us distinctly what to do as to it; He has said, "Search!" Now, are we substituting a word of

Margin references: 2 Timothy 3:17 / 1 Thess. 2:13 / 2 Peter 1:3, 4 / 1 Peter 1:8 / John 5:39 / Luke 24:27 / John 16:15 / Ephesians 4:13 / John 6:63 / Colossians 3:16 / Luke 2:14 / John 17:14 / John 5:39

Isaiah 34:16

our own, and merely *reading* them? He did not say, "Read them," but "*Search!*" and it is a most serious thought for many a comfortable daily *reader* of the Bible, that, if they are *only* reading and not searching, they are distinctly living in disobedience to one of His plainest commands. What wonder if they do not "grow thereby"!

> Let me then be always growing,
>   Never, never standing still,
> Listening, learning, better knowing
>   Thee, and Thy most blessed will;
> That the Master's eye may trace,
> Day by day, my growth in grace.

The Scripture Cannot Be Broken.

John 10:35.

Upon the Word I rest,
    Each pilgrim day;
This golden staff is best
    For all the way.
What Jesus Christ hath spoken,
    Can*not* be broken!

Upon the Word I rest,
    So strong, so sure,
So full of comfort blest,
    So sweet, so pure!
The charter of salvation,
    Faith's broad foundation.

Upon the Word I stand!
    That cannot die!
Christ seals it in my hand,
    He cannot lie!
The word that faileth never!
    Abiding ever!

Chorus. The Master hath said it! Rejoicing in this,
    We ask not for sign or for token;
His word is enough for our confident bliss,—
    'The Scripture *cannot* be broken!'

Frances Ridley Havergal

Painted by Hope J.Stewart, from a Sketch by the late R.M.M'Cheyne, Æt. 21. — Engd by J.Le Conte, Edinr

Ever your till glory

Robt. Murray M'Cheyne.

Robert Murray Mʻ Cheyne (1813–1843)

ROBERT MURRAY M'CHEYNE'S BIBLE READING CALENDAR.

R. M. M'Cheyne (1813–1843) was the minister of
St. Peter's Church, Dundee, Scotland.

DAILY BREAD.

BEING A CALENDAR FOR READING THROUGH THE WORD OF GOD IN A YEAR.

*"Thy Word is very pure; therefore
Thy servant loveth it."*

MY DEAR FLOCK,—The approach of another year stirs up within me new desires for your salvation, and for the growth of those of you who are saved. "God is my record how greatly I long after you all in the bowels of Jesus Christ." What the coming year is to bring forth, who can tell? There is plainly a weight lying on the spirits of all good men, and a looking for some strange work of judgment upon this land. There is a need now to ask that solemn question—"If in the land of peace wherein thou trustedst, they wearied thee, then how wilt thou do in the swelling of Jordan?"

Those believers will stand firmest who have no dependence upon self or upon creatures, but upon Jehovah our Righteousness. We must be driven more to our Bibles, and to the mercy-seat, if we are to stand in the evil day. Then we shall be able to say, like David—"The proud have had me greatly in derision, yet have I not declined from Thy law." "Princes have persecuted me without a cause, but my heart standeth in awe of Thy word."

It has long been in my mind to prepare a scheme of Scripture reading, in which as many as were made willing by God might agree, so that the whole Bible might be read once by you in the year, and all might be feeding in the same portion of the green pasture at the same time.

I am quite aware that such a plan is accompanied with many

DANGERS.

(1.) *Formality.*—We are such weak creatures that any regularly returning duty is apt to degenerate into a lifeless form. The tendency of reading the Word by a fixed rule may, in some minds, be to create this skeleton religion. This is to be the peculiar sin of the last days—"Having a form of godliness, but denying the power thereof." Guard against this. Let the calendar perish rather than this rust eat up your souls.

(2.) *Self-righteousness.*—Some, when they have devoted their set time to reading of the Word, and accomplished their prescribed portion, may be tempted to look at themselves with self-complacency. Many, I am persuaded, are living without any Divine work on their soul—unpardoned and unsanctified, and ready to perish—who spend their appointed times in secret and family devotion. This is going to hell with a lie in their right hand.

(3.) *Careless reading.*—Few *tremble* at the Word of God. Few, in reading it, hear the voice of Jehovah, which is full of majesty. Some, by having so large a portion, may be tempted to weary of it, as Israel did of the daily manna, saying—"Our soul loatheth this light bread"; and to read it in a slight and careless manner. This would be fearfully provoking to God. Take heed lest that word be true of you—"Ye said, also, Behold what a weariness is it! and ye have snuffed at it, saith the Lord of Hosts."

(4.) *A yoke too heavy to bear.* Some may engage in reading with alacrity for a time, and afterwards feel it a burden, grievous to be borne. They may find conscience dragging them through the appointed task without any relish of the heavenly food. If this be the case with any, throw aside the fetter, and feed at liberty in the sweet garden of God. My desire is not to cast a snare upon you, but to be a helper of your joy.

If there be so many dangers, why propose such a scheme at all? To this I answer, that the best things are accompanied with danger, as the fairest flowers are often gathered in the clefts of some dangerous precipice. Let us weigh

THE ADVANTAGES.

(1.) The whole Bible will be read through in an orderly manner in the course of a year.—The Old Testament once, the New Testament and Psalms twice. I fear many of you never read the whole Bible; and yet it is all equally Divine, "All Scripture is given by inspiration of God, and is profitable for doctrine, for reproof, for correction, and instruction in righteousness, that the man of God may be perfect." If we pass over some parts of Scripture, we shall be incomplete Christians.

(2.) Time will not be wasted in choosing what portions to read. Often believers are at a loss to determine towards which part of the mountains of spices they should bend their steps. Here the question will be solved at once in a very simple manner.

(3.) Parents will have a regular subject upon which to examine their children and servants.—It is much to be desired that family worship were made more instructive than it generally is. The mere reading of the chapter is often too like water spilt on the ground. Let it be read by every member of the family before-hand, and then the meaning and application drawn out by simple question and answer. The calendar will be helpful in this. Friends, also, when they meet, will have a subject for profitable conversation in the portions read that day. The meaning of difficult passages may be inquired from the more judicious and ripe Christians, and the fragrance of simpler Scriptures spread abroad.

(4.) The pastor will know in what part of the pasture the flock are feeding.— He will thus be enabled to speak more suitably to them on the Sabbath; and both pastor and elders will be able to drop a word of light and comfort in visiting from house to house, which will be more readily responded to.

(5.) The sweet bond of Christian love and unity will be strengthened.—We shall be often led to think of those dear brothers and sisters in the Lord, here and elsewhere, who agree to join with us in reading those portions. We shall oftener be led to agree on earth, touching something we shall ask of God. We shall pray over the same promises, mourn over the same confessions, praise God in the same songs, and be nourished by the same words of eternal life.

DIRECTIONS FOR M'CHEYNE'S DAILY BIBLE READING.

1. The centre columns contains the day of the month. The left hand columns contain the chapter to be read in the family. The right hand columns contain the portions to be read in secret.

2. The head of the family should previously read over the chapter indicated for the family worship and mark two or three of the most prominent verses upon which he may dwell, asking a few simple questions.

3. Frequently the chapter named in the calendar for family reading might be read more suitably in secret; in which case the head of the family should intimate that it be read in private, and the chapter for secret reading may be used in the family.

4. The metrical version of the Psalms should be read or sung through at least once in the year. It is truly an admirable translation from the Hebrew, and is frequently more correct than the prose version.
   (If three verses be sung at each diet of family worship, the whole Psalms will be sung through in the year.)

5. Let the conversation at the family meals frequently turn upon the chapter read; thus every meal will be a sacrament, being sanctified by the Word and prayer.

6. Let our secret reading prevent the dawning of the day. Let God's voice be the first we hear in the morning. Mark two or three of the richest verses and pray over every line and word of them.
   (Let the marks be neatly done, never as to abuse a copy of the Bible.)

7. In meeting believers on the street or elsewhere, when an easy opportunity offers, recur to the chapters read that morning. This will be a blessed exchange for those idle words which waste the soul and grieve the Holy Spirit of God.
   (In writing letters to those at a distance, make use of the provision of the day gathered.)

8. Above all, use the Word as a lamp to your feet and a light to your path— your guide in perplexity, your armour in temptation, your food in times of faintness. Hear the constant cry of the great Intercessor,

"SANCTIFY THEM THROUGH THY TRUTH: THY WORD IS TRUTH."

St. Peter's, Dundee, December 30, 1842.

JANUARY/FAMILY   *This is my beloved Son, in whom*

Book	Chapter	Book	Chapter	JANUARY
Genesis	1	Matthew	1	1
Genesis	2	Matthew	2	2
Genesis	3	Matthew	3	3
Genesis	4	Matthew	4	4
Genesis	5	Matthew	5	5
Genesis	6	Matthew	6	6
Genesis	7	Matthew	7	7
Genesis	8	Matthew	8	8
Genesis	9, 10	Matthew	9	9
Genesis	11	Matthew	10	10
Genesis	12	Matthew	11	11
Genesis	13	Matthew	12	12
Genesis	14	Matthew	13	13
Genesis	15	Matthew	14	14
Genesis	16	Matthew	15	15
Genesis	17	Matthew	16	16
Genesis	18	Matthew	17	17
Genesis	19	Matthew	18	18
Genesis	20	Matthew	19	19
Genesis	21	Matthew	20	20
Genesis	22	Matthew	21	21
Genesis	23	Matthew	22	22
Genesis	24	Matthew	23	23
Genesis	25	Matthew	24	24
Genesis	26	Matthew	25	25
Genesis	27	Matthew	26	26
Genesis	28	Matthew	27	27
Genesis	29	Matthew	28	28
Genesis	30	Mark	1	29
Genesis	31	Mark	2	30
Genesis	32	Mark	3	31

I am well pleased; hear ye him.

January	Book	Chapter	Book	Chapter
1	Ezra	1	Acts	1
2	Ezra	2	Acts	2
3	Ezra	3	Acts	3
4	Ezra	4	Acts	4
5	Ezra	5	Acts	5
6	Ezra	6	Acts	6
7	Ezra	7	Acts	7
8	Ezra	8	Acts	8
9	Ezra	9	Acts	9
10	Ezra	10	Acts	10
11	Nehemiah	1	Acts	11
12	Nehemiah	2	Acts	12
13	Nehemiah	3	Acts	13
14	Nehemiah	4	Acts	14
15	Nehemiah	5	Acts	15
16	Nehemiah	6	Acts	16
17	Nehemiah	7	Acts	17
18	Nehemiah	8	Acts	18
19	Nehemiah	9	Acts	19
20	Nehemiah	10	Acts	20
21	Nehemiah	11	Acts	21
22	Nehemiah	12	Acts	22
23	Nehemiah	13	Acts	23
24	Esther	1	Acts	24
25	Esther	2	Acts	25
26	Esther	3	Acts	26
27	Esther	4	Acts	27
28	Esther	5	Acts	28
29	Esther	6	Romans	1
30	Esther	7	Romans	2
31	Esther	8	Romans	3

Book	Chapter	Book	Chapter	FEBRUARY
Genesis	33	Mark	4	1
Genesis	34	Mark	5	2
Genesis	35, 36	Mark	6	3
Genesis	37	Mark	7	4
Genesis	38	Mark	8	5
Genesis	39	Mark	9	6
Genesis	40	Mark	10	7
Genesis	41	Mark	11	8
Genesis	42	Mark	12	9
Genesis	43	Mark	13	10
Genesis	44	Mark	14	11
Genesis	45	Mark	15	12
Genesis	46	Mark	16	13
Genesis	47	Luke	1:1–38	14
Genesis	48	Luke	1:39–80	15
Genesis	49	Luke	2	16
Genesis	50	Luke	3	17
Exodus	1	Luke	4	18
Exodus	2	Luke	5	19
Exodus	3	Luke	6	20
Exodus	4	Luke	7	21
Exodus	5	Luke	8	22
Exodus	6	Luke	9	23
Exodus	7	Luke	10	24
Exodus	8	Luke	11	25
Exodus	9	Luke	12	26
Exodus	10	Luke	13	27
Exodus	11, 12:1–21	Luke	14	28

mouth more than my necessary food.   Secret/February

February	Book	Chapter	Book	Chapter
1	Esther	9 , 10	Romans	4
2	Job	1	Romans	5
3	Job	2	Romans	6
4	Job	3	Romans	7
5	Job	4	Romans	8
6	Job	5	Romans	9
7	Job	6	Romans	10
8	Job	7	Romans	11
9	Job	8	Romans	12
10	Job	9	Romans	13
11	Job	10	Romans	14
12	Job	11	Romans	15
13	Job	12	Romans	16
14	Job	13	1 Corinthians	1
15	Job	14	1 Corinthians	2
16	Job	15	1 Corinthians	3
17	Job	16, 17	1 Corinthians	4
18	Job	18	1 Corinthians	5
19	Job	19	1 Corinthians	6
20	Job	20	1 Corinthians	7
21	Job	21	1 Corinthians	8
22	Job	22	1 Corinthians	9
23	Job	23	1 Corinthians	10
24	Job	24	1 Corinthians	11
25	Job	25, 26	1 Corinthians	12
26	Job	27	1 Corinthians	13
27	Job	28	1 Corinthians	14
28	Job	29	1 Corinthians	15

MARCH/FAMILY   *Mary kept all these things, and*

Book	Chapter	Book	Chapter	MARCH
Exodus	12:22–51	Luke	15	1
Exodus	13	Luke	16	2
Exodus	14	Luke	17	3
Exodus	15	Luke	18	4
Exodus	16	Luke	19	5
Exodus	17	Luke	20	6
Exodus	18	Luke	21	7
Exodus	19	Luke	22	8
Exodus	20	Luke	23	9
Exodus	21	Luke	24	10
Exodus	22	John	1	11
Exodus	23	John	2	12
Exodus	24	John	3	13
Exodus	25	John	4	14
Exodus	26	John	5	15
Exodus	27	John	6	16
Exodus	28	John	7	17
Exodus	29	John	8	18
Exodus	30	John	9	19
Exodus	31	John	10	20
Exodus	32	John	11	21
Exodus	33	John	12	22
Exodus	34	John	13	23
Exodus	35	John	14	24
Exodus	36	John	15	25
Exodus	37	John	16	26
Exodus	38	John	17	27
Exodus	39	John	18	28
Exodus	40	John	19	29
Leviticus	1	John	20	30
Leviticus	2, 3	John	21	31

pondered them in her heart.   Secret/March

March	Book	Chapter	Book	Chapter
1	Job	30	1 Corinthians	16
2	Job	31	2 Corinthians	1
3	Job	32	2 Corinthians	2
4	Job	33	2 Corinthians	3
5	Job	34	2 Corinthians	4
6	Job	35	2 Corinthians	1
7	Job	36	2 Corinthians	6
8	Job	37	2 Corinthians	7
9	Job	38	2 Corinthians	8
10	Job	39	2 Corinthians	9
11	Job	40	2 Corinthians	10
12	Job	41	2 Corinthians	11
13	Job	42	2 Corinthians	12
14	Proverbs	1	2 Corinthians	13
15	Proverbs	2	Galatians	1
16	Proverbs	3	Galatians	2
17	Proverbs	4	Galatians	3
18	Proverbs	5	Galatians	4
19	Proverbs	6	Galatians	5
20	Proverbs	7	Galatians	6
21	Proverbs	8	Ephesians	1
22	Proverbs	9	Ephesians	2
23	Proverbs	10	Ephesians	3
24	Proverbs	11	Ephesians	4
25	Proverbs	12	Ephesians	5
26	Proverbs	13	Ephesians	6
27	Proverbs	14	Philippians	1
28	Proverbs	15	Philippians	2
29	Proverbs	16	Philippians	3
30	Proverbs	17	Philippians	4
31	Proverbs	18	Colossians	1

APRIL/FAMILY   *O send out thy light and thy*

Book	Chapter	Book	Chapter	APRIL
Leviticus	4	Psalms	1 , 2	1
Leviticus	5	Psalms	3 , 4	2
Leviticus	6	Psalms	5 , 6	3
Leviticus	7	Psalms	7 , 8	4
Leviticus	8	Psalms	9	5
Leviticus	9	Psalms	10	6
Leviticus	10	Psalms	11, 12	7
Leviticus	11, 12	Psalms	13, 14	8
Leviticus	13	Psalms	15, 16	9
Leviticus	14	Psalms	17	10
Leviticus	15	Psalms	18	11
Leviticus	16	Psalms	19	12
Leviticus	17	Psalms	20, 21	13
Leviticus	18	Psalms	22	14
Leviticus	19	Psalms	23, 24	15
Leviticus	20	Psalms	25	16
Leviticus	21	Psalms	26, 27	17
Leviticus	22	Psalms	28, 29	18
Leviticus	23	Psalms	30	19
Leviticus	24	Psalms	31	20
Leviticus	25	Psalms	32	21
Leviticus	26	Psalms	33	22
Leviticus	27	Psalms	34	23
Numbers	1	Psalms	35	24
Numbers	2	Psalms	36	25
Numbers	3	Psalms	37	26
Numbers	4	Psalms	38	27
Numbers	5	Psalms	39	28
Numbers	6	Psalms	40, 41	29
Numbers	7	Psalms	42, 43	30

truth; let them lead me.   SECRET/APRIL

APRIL	Book	Chapter	Book	Chapter
1	Proverbs	19	Colossians	2
2	Proverbs	20	Colossians	3
3	Proverbs	21	Colossians	4
4	Proverbs	22	1 Thessalonians	1
5	Proverbs	23	1 Thessalonians	2
6	Proverbs	24	1 Thessalonians	3
7	Proverbs	25	1 Thessalonians	4
8	Proverbs	26	1 Thessalonians	5
9	Proverbs	27	2 Thessalonians	1
10	Proverbs	28	2 Thessalonians	2
11	Proverbs	29	2 Thessalonians	3
12	Proverbs	30	1 Timothy	1
13	Proverbs	31	1 Timothy	2
14	Ecclesiastes	1	1 Timothy	3
15	Ecclesiastes	2	1 Timothy	4
16	Ecclesiastes	3	1 Timothy	5
17	Ecclesiastes	4	1 Timothy	6
18	Ecclesiastes	5	2 Timothy	1
19	Ecclesiastes	6	2 Timothy	2
20	Ecclesiastes	7	2 Timothy	3
21	Ecclesiastes	8	2 Timothy	4
22	Ecclesiastes	9	Titus	1
23	Ecclesiastes	10	Titus	2
24	Ecclesiastes	11	Titus	3
25	Ecclesiastes	12	Philemon	1
26	Song	1	Hebrews	1
27	Song	2	Hebrews	2
28	Song	3	Hebrews	3
29	Song	4	Hebrews	4
30	Song	5	Hebrews	5

MAY/FAMILY   *From a child thou hast*

Book	Chapter	Book	Chapter	MAY
Numbers	8	Psalms	44	1
Numbers	9	Psalms	45	2
Numbers	10	Psalms	46, 47	3
Numbers	11	Psalms	48	4
Numbers	12, 13	Psalms	49	5
Numbers	14	Psalms	50	6
Numbers	15	Psalms	51	7
Numbers	16	Psalms	52, 53, 54	8
Numbers	17, 18	Psalms	55	9
Numbers	19	Psalms	56, 57	10
Numbers	20	Psalms	58, 59	11
Numbers	21	Psalms	60, 61	12
Numbers	22	Psalms	62, 63	13
Numbers	23	Psalms	64, 65	14
Numbers	24	Psalms	66, 67	15
Numbers	25	Psalms	68	16
Numbers	26	Psalms	69	17
Numbers	27	Psalms	70, 71	18
Numbers	28	Psalms	72	19
Numbers	29	Psalms	73	20
Numbers	30	Psalms	74	21
Numbers	31	Psalms	75, 76	22
Numbers	32	Psalms	77	23
Numbers	33	Psalms	78:1–37	24
Numbers	34	Psalms	78:38–72	25
Numbers	35	Psalms	79	26
Numbers	36	Psalms	80	27
Deuteronomy	1	Psalms	81, 82	28
Deuteronomy	2	Psalms	83, 84	29
Deuteronomy	3	Psalms	85	30
Deuteronomy	4	Psalms	86, 87	31

known the holy Scriptures.   SECRET/MAY

MAY	Book	Chapter	Book	Chapter
1	Song	6	Hebrews	6
2	Song	7	Hebrews	7
3	Song	8	Hebrews	8
4	Isaiah	1	Hebrews	9
5	Isaiah	2	Hebrews	10
6	Isaiah	3, 4	Hebrews	11
7	Isaiah	5	Hebrews	12
8	Isaiah	6	Hebrews	13
9	Isaiah	7	James	1
10	Isaiah	8, 9:1–7	James	2
11	Isaiah	9:7–21; 10:1–4	James	3
12	Isaiah	10:5–34	James	4
13	Isaiah	11 , 12	James	5
14	Isaiah	13	1 Peter	1
15	Isaiah	14	1 Peter	2
16	Isaiah	15	1 Peter	3
17	Isaiah	16	1 Peter	4
18	Isaiah	17, 18	1 Peter	5
19	Isaiah	19, 20	2 Peter	1
20	Isaiah	21	2 Peter	2
21	Isaiah	22	2 Peter	3
22	Isaiah	23	1 John	1
23	Isaiah	24	1 John	2
24	Isaiah	25	1 John	3
25	Isaiah	26	1 John	4
26	Isaiah	27	1 John	5
27	Isaiah	28	2 John	1
28	Isaiah	29	3 John	1
29	Isaiah	30	Jude	1
30	Isaiah	31	Revelation	1
31	Isaiah	32	Revelation	2

JUNE/FAMILY   *Blessed is he that readeth*

Book	Chapter	Book	Chapter	JUNE
Deuteronomy	5	Psalms	88	1
Deuteronomy	6	Psalms	89	2
Deuteronomy	7	Psalms	90	3
Deuteronomy	8	Psalms	91	4
Deuteronomy	9	Psalms	92, 93	5
Deuteronomy	10	Psalms	94	6
Deuteronomy	11	Psalms	95, 96	7
Deuteronomy	12	Psalms	97, 98	8
Deuteronomy	13, 14	Psalms	99, 100, 101	9
Deuteronomy	15	Psalms	102	10
Deuteronomy	16	Psalms	103	11
Deuteronomy	17	Psalms	104	12
Deuteronomy	18	Psalms	105	13
Deuteronomy	19	Psalms	106	14
Deuteronomy	20	Psalms	107	15
Deuteronomy	21	Psalms	108, 109	16
Deuteronomy	22	Psalms	110, 111	17
Deuteronomy	23	Psalms	112, 113	18
Deuteronomy	24	Psalms	114, 115	19
Deuteronomy	25	Psalms	116	20
Deuteronomy	26	Psalms	117, 118	21
Deuteronomy	27, 28:1–19	Psalms	119:1–24	22
Deuteronomy	28:20–68	Psalms	119:25–48	23
Deuteronomy	29	Psalms	119:49–72	24
Deuteronomy	30	Psalms	119:73–96	25
Deuteronomy	31	Psalms	119:97–120	26
Deuteronomy	32	Psalms	119:121–144	27
Deuteronomy	33, 34	Psalms	119:145–176	28
Joshua	1	Psalms	120, 121, 122	29
Joshua	2	Psalms	123, 124, 125	30

and they that hear.

JUNE	Book	Chapter	Book	Chapter
1	Isaiah	33	Revelation	3
2	Isaiah	34	Revelation	4
3	Isaiah	35	Revelation	5
4	Isaiah	36	Revelation	6
5	Isaiah	37	Revelation	7
6	Isaiah	38	Revelation	8
7	Isaiah	39	Revelation	9
8	Isaiah	40	Revelation	10
9	Isaiah	41	Revelation	11
10	Isaiah	42	Revelation	12
11	Isaiah	43	Revelation	13
12	Isaiah	44	Revelation	14
13	Isaiah	45	Revelation	15
14	Isaiah	46	Revelation	16
15	Isaiah	47	Revelation	17
16	Isaiah	48	Revelation	18
17	Isaiah	49	Revelation	19
18	Isaiah	50	Revelation	20
19	Isaiah	51	Revelation	21
20	Isaiah	52	Revelation	22
21	Isaiah	53	Matthew	1
22	Isaiah	54	Matthew	2
23	Isaiah	55	Matthew	3
24	Isaiah	56	Matthew	4
25	Isaiah	57	Matthew	5
26	Isaiah	58	Matthew	6
27	Isaiah	59	Matthew	7
28	Isaiah	60	Matthew	8
29	Isaiah	61	Matthew	9
30	Isaiah	62	Matthew	10

They received the word with all readiness

Book	Chapter	Book	Chapter	July
Joshua	3	Psalms	126, 127, 128	1
Joshua	4	Psalms	129, 130, 131	2
Joshua	5, 6:1–5	Psalms	132, 133, 134	3
Joshua	6:6–27	Psalms	135, 136	4
Joshua	7	Psalms	137, 138	5
Joshua	8	Psalms	139	6
Joshua	9	Psalms	140, 141	7
Joshua	10	Psalms	142, 143	8
Joshua	11	Psalms	144	9
Joshua	12, 13	Psalms	145	10
Joshua	14, 15	Psalms	146, 147	11
Joshua	16, 17	Psalms	148	12
Joshua	18, 19	Psalms	149, 150	13
Joshua	20, 21	Acts	1	14
Joshua	22	Acts	2	15
Joshua	23	Acts	3	16
Joshua	24	Acts	4	17
Judges	1	Acts	5	18
Judges	2	Acts	6	19
Judges	3	Acts	7	20
Judges	4	Acts	8	21
Judges	5	Acts	9	22
Judges	6	Acts	10	23
Judges	7	Acts	11	24
Judges	8	Acts	12	25
Judges	9	Acts	13	26
Judges	10, 11:1–11	Acts	14	27
Judges	11:12–40	Acts	15	28
Judges	12	Acts	16	29
Judges	13	Acts	17	30
Judges	14	Acts	18	31

of mind, and searched the Scriptures daily.   SECRET/JULY

JULY	Book	Chapter	Book	Chapter
1	Isaiah	63	Matthew	11
2	Isaiah	64	Matthew	12
3	Isaiah	65	Matthew	13
4	Isaiah	66	Matthew	14
5	Jeremiah	1	Matthew	15
6	Jeremiah	2	Matthew	16
7	Jeremiah	3	Matthew	17
8	Jeremiah	4	Matthew	18
9	Jeremiah	5	Matthew	19
10	Jeremiah	6	Matthew	20
11	Jeremiah	7	Matthew	21
12	Jeremiah	8	Matthew	22
13	Jeremiah	9	Matthew	23
14	Jeremiah	10	Matthew	24
15	Jeremiah	11	Matthew	25
16	Jeremiah	12	Matthew	26
17	Jeremiah	13	Matthew	27
18	Jeremiah	14	Matthew	28
19	Jeremiah	15	Mark	1
20	Jeremiah	16	Mark	2
21	Jeremiah	17	Mark	3
22	Jeremiah	18	Mark	4
23	Jeremiah	19	Mark	5
24	Jeremiah	20	Mark	6
25	Jeremiah	21	Mark	7
26	Jeremiah	22	Mark	8
27	Jeremiah	23	Mark	9
28	Jeremiah	24	Mark	10
29	Jeremiah	25	Mark	11
30	Jeremiah	26	Mark	12
31	Jeremiah	27	Mark	13

Book	Chapter	Book	Chapter	AUGUST
Judges	15	Acts	19	1
Judges	16	Acts	20	2
Judges	17	Acts	21	3
Judges	18	Acts	22	4
Judges	19	Acts	23	5
Judges	20	Acts	24	6
Judges	21	Acts	25	7
Ruth	1	Acts	26	8
Ruth	2	Acts	27	9
Ruth	3, 4	Acts	28	10
1 Samuel	1	Romans	1	11
1 Samuel	2	Romans	2	12
1 Samuel	3	Romans	3	13
1 Samuel	4	Romans	4	14
1 Samuel	5, 6	Romans	5	15
1 Samuel	7, 8	Romans	6	16
1 Samuel	9	Romans	7	17
1 Samuel	10	Romans	8	18
1 Samuel	11	Romans	9	19
1 Samuel	12	Romans	10	20
1 Samuel	13	Romans	11	21
1 Samuel	14	Romans	12	22
1 Samuel	15	Romans	13	23
1 Samuel	16	Romans	14	24
1 Samuel	17	Romans	15	25
1 Samuel	18	Romans	16	26
1 Samuel	19	1 Corinthians	1	27
1 Samuel	20	1 Corinthians	2	28
1 Samuel	21, 22	1 Corinthians	3	29
1 Samuel	23	1 Corinthians	4	30
1 Samuel	24	1 Corinthians	5	31

thy servant heareth.   SECRET/AUGUST

AUGUST	Book	Chapter	Book	Chapter
1	Jeremiah	28	Mark	14
2	Jeremiah	29	Mark	15
3	Jeremiah	30, 31	Mark	16
4	Jeremiah	32	Psalms	1, 2
5	Jeremiah	33	Psalms	3, 4
6	Jeremiah	34	Psalms	5, 6
7	Jeremiah	35	Psalms	7, 8
8	Jeremiah	36	Psalms	9
9	Jeremiah	37	Psalms	10
10	Jeremiah	38	Psalms	11, 12
11	Jeremiah	39	Psalms	13, 14
12	Jeremiah	40	Psalms	15, 16
13	Jeremiah	41	Psalms	17
14	Jeremiah	42	Psalms	18
15	Jeremiah	43	Psalms	19
16	Jeremiah	44, 45	Psalms	20, 21
17	Jeremiah	46	Psalms	22
18	Jeremiah	47	Psalms	23, 24
19	Jeremiah	48	Psalms	25
20	Jeremiah	49	Psalms	26, 27
21	Jeremiah	50	Psalms	28, 29
22	Jeremiah	51	Psalms	30
23	Jeremiah	52	Psalms	31
24	Lamentations	1	Psalms	32
25	Lamentations	2	Psalms	33
26	Lamentations	3	Psalms	34
27	Lamentations	4	Psalms	35
28	Lamentations	5	Psalms	36
29	Ezekiel	1	Psalms	37
30	Ezekiel	2	Psalms	38
31	Ezekiel	3	Psalms	39

SEPTEMBER/FAMILY   *The Law of the Lord is perfect,*

Book	Chapter	Book	Chapter	SEPTEMBER
1 Samuel	25	1 Corinthians	6	1
1 Samuel	26	1 Corinthians	7	2
1 Samuel	27	1 Corinthians	8	3
1 Samuel	28	1 Corinthians	9	4
1 Samuel	29, 30	1 Corinthians	10	5
1 Samuel	31	1 Corinthians	11	6
2 Samuel	1	1 Corinthians	12	7
2 Samuel	2	1 Corinthians	13	8
2 Samuel	3	1 Corinthians	14	9
2 Samuel	4, 5	1 Corinthians	15	10
2 Samuel	6	1 Corinthians	16	11
2 Samuel	7	2 Corinthians	1	12
2 Samuel	8, 9	2 Corinthians	2	13
2 Samuel	10	2 Corinthians	3	14
2 Samuel	11	2 Corinthians	4	15
2 Samuel	12	2 Corinthians	5	16
2 Samuel	13	2 Corinthians	6	17
2 Samuel	14	2 Corinthians	7	18
2 Samuel	15	2 Corinthians	8	19
2 Samuel	16	2 Corinthians	9	20
2 Samuel	17	2 Corinthians	10	21
2 Samuel	18	2 Corinthians	11	22
2 Samuel	19	2 Corinthians	12	23
2 Samuel	20	2 Corinthians	13	24
2 Samuel	21	Galatians	1	25
2 Samuel	22	Galatians	2	26
2 Samuel	23	Galatians	3	27
2 Samuel	24	Galatians	4	28
1 Kings	1	Galatians	5	29
1 Kings	2	Galatians	6	30

converting the soul.

SEPTEMBER	Book	Chapter	Book	Chapter
1	Ezekiel	4	Psalms	40, 41
2	Ezekiel	5	Psalms	42, 43
3	Ezekiel	6	Psalms	44
4	Ezekiel	7	Psalms	45
5	Ezekiel	8	Psalms	46, 47
6	Ezekiel	9	Psalms	48
7	Ezekiel	10	Psalms	49
8	Ezekiel	11	Psalms	50
9	Ezekiel	12	Psalms	51
10	Ezekiel	13	Psalms	52, 53, 54
11	Ezekiel	14	Psalms	55
12	Ezekiel	15	Psalms	56, 57
13	Ezekiel	16	Psalms	58, 59
14	Ezekiel	17	Psalms	60, 61
15	Ezekiel	18	Psalms	62, 63
16	Ezekiel	19	Psalms	64, 65
17	Ezekiel	20	Psalms	66, 67
18	Ezekiel	21	Psalms	68
19	Ezekiel	22	Psalms	69
20	Ezekiel	23	Psalms	70, 71
21	Ezekiel	24	Psalms	72
22	Ezekiel	25	Psalms	73
23	Ezekiel	26	Psalms	74
24	Ezekiel	27	Psalms	75, 76
25	Ezekiel	28	Psalms	77
26	Ezekiel	29	Psalms	78:1–37
27	Ezekiel	30	Psalms	78:38–72
28	Ezekiel	31	Psalms	79
29	Ezekiel	32	Psalms	80
30	Ezekiel	33	Psalms	81, 82

OCTOBER/FAMILY   *O how I love thy law! It is*

Book	Chapter	Book	Chapter	OCTOBER
1 Kings	3	Ephesians	1	1
1 Kings	4, 5	Ephesians	2	2
1 Kings	6	Ephesians	3	3
1 Kings	7	Ephesians	4	4
1 Kings	8	Ephesians	5	5
1 Kings	9	Ephesians	6	6
1 Kings	10	Phillipians	1	7
1 Kings	11	Phillipians	2	8
1 Kings	12	Phillipians	3	9
1 Kings	13	Phillipians	4	10
1 Kings	14	Colossians	1	11
1 Kings	15	Colossians	2	12
1 Kings	16	Colossians	3	13
1 Kings	17	Colossians	4	14
1 Kings	18	1 Thessalonians	1	15
1 Kings	19	1 Thessalonians	2	16
1 Kings	20	1 Thessalonians	3	17
1 Kings	21	1 Thessalonians	4	18
1 Kings	22	1 Thessalonians	5	19
2 Kings	1	2 Thessalonians	1	20
2 Kings	2	2 Thessalonians	2	21
2 Kings	3	2 Thessalonians	3	22
2 Kings	4	1 Timothy	1	23
2 Kings	5	1 Timothy	2	24
2 Kings	6	1 Timothy	3	25
2 Kings	7	1 Timothy	4	26
2 Kings	8	1 Timothy	5	27
2 Kings	9	1 Timothy	6	28
2 Kings	10	2 Timothy	1	29
2 Kings	11, 12	2 Timothy	2	30
2 Kings	13	2 Timothy	3	31

my meditation all the day.

OCTOBER	Book	Chapter	Book	Chapter
1	Ezekiel	34	Psalms	83, 84
2	Ezekiel	35	Psalms	85
3	Ezekiel	36	Psalms	86
4	Ezekiel	37	Psalms	87, 88
5	Ezekiel	38	Psalms	89
6	Ezekiel	39	Psalms	90
7	Ezekiel	40	Psalms	91
8	Ezekiel	41	Psalms	92, 93
9	Ezekiel	42	Psalms	94
10	Ezekiel	43	Psalms	95, 96
11	Ezekiel	44	Psalms	97, 98
12	Ezekiel	45	Psalms	99, 100, 101
13	Ezekiel	46	Psalms	102
14	Ezekiel	47	Psalms	103
15	Ezekiel	48	Psalms	104
16	Daniel	1	Psalms	105
17	Daniel	2	Psalms	106
18	Daniel	3	Psalms	107
19	Daniel	4	Psalms	108, 109
20	Daniel	5	Psalms	110, 111
21	Daniel	6	Psalms	112, 113
22	Daniel	7	Psalms	114, 115
23	Daniel	8	Psalms	116
24	Daniel	9	Psalms	117, 118
25	Daniel	10	Psalms	119:1–24
26	Daniel	11	Psalms	119:25–48
27	Daniel	12	Psalms	119:49–72
28	Hosea	1	Psalms	119:73–96
29	Hosea	2	Psalms	119:97–120
30	Hosea	3, 4	Psalms	119:121–144
31	Hosea	5, 6	Psalms	119:145–176

NOVEMBER/FAMILY   *As new-born babes, desire the sincere milk*

Book	Chapter	Book	Chapter	NOVEMBER
2 Kings	14	2 Timothy	4	1
2 Kings	15	Titus	1	2
2 Kings	16	Titus	2	3
2 Kings	17	Titus	3	4
2 Kings	18	Philemon	1	5
2 Kings	19	Hebrews	1	6
2 Kings	20	Hebrews	2	7
2 Kings	21	Hebrews	3	8
2 Kings	22	Hebrews	4	9
2 Kings	23	Hebrews	5	10
2 Kings	24	Hebrews	6	11
2 Kings	25	Hebrews	7	12
1 Chronicles	1, 2	Hebrews	8	13
1 Chronicles	3, 4	Hebrews	9	14
1 Chronicles	5, 6	Hebrews	10	15
1 Chronicles	7, 8	Hebrews	11	16
1 Chronicles	9, 10	Hebrews	12	17
1 Chronicles	11, 12	Hebrews	13	18
1 Chronicles	13, 14	James	1	19
1 Chronicles	15	James	2	20
1 Chronicles	16	James	3	21
1 Chronicles	17	James	4	22
1 Chronicles	18	James	5	23
1 Chronicles	19, 20	1 Peter	1	24
1 Chronicles	21	1 Peter	2	25
1 Chronicles	22	1 Peter	3	26
1 Chronicles	23	1 Peter	4	27
1 Chronicles	24, 25	1 Peter	5	28
1 Chronicles	26, 27	2 Peter	1	29
1 Chronicles	28	2 Peter	2	30

of the word, that ye may grow thereby.   SECRET/NOVEMBER

NOVEMBER	Book	Chapter	Book	Chapter
1	Hosea	7	Psalms	120, 121, 122
2	Hosea	8	Psalms	123, 124, 125
3	Hosea	9	Psalms	126, 127, 128
4	Hosea	10	Psalms	129, 130, 131
5	Hosea	11	Psalms	132, 133, 134
6	Hosea	12	Psalms	135, 136
7	Hosea	13	Psalms	137, 138
8	Hosea	14	Psalms	139
9	Joel	1	Psalms	140, 141
10	Joel	2	Psalms	142
11	Joel	3	Psalms	143
12	Amos	1	Psalms	144
13	Amos	2	Psalms	145
14	Amos	3	Psalms	146, 147
15	Amos	4	Psalms	148, 149, 150
16	Amos	5	Luke	1:1–38
17	Amos	6	Luke	1:39–80
18	Amos	7	Luke	2
19	Amos	8	Luke	3
20	Amos	9	Luke	4
21	Obadiah	1	Luke	5
22	Jonah	1	Luke	6
23	Jonah	2	Luke	7
24	Jonah	3	Luke	8
25	Jonah	4	Luke	9
26	Micah	1	Luke	10
27	Micah	2	Luke	11
28	Micah	3	Luke	12
29	Micah	4	Luke	13
30	Micah	5	Luke	14

DECEMBER/FAMILY   *The law of his God is in his heart;*

Book	Chapter	Book	Chapter	DECEMBER
1 Chronicles	29	2 Peter	3	1
2 Chronicles	1	1 John	1	2
2 Chronicles	2	1 John	2	3
2 Chronicles	3 , 4	1 John	3	4
2 Chronicles	5, 6:1–11	1 John	4	5
2 Chronicles	6:12–42	1 John	5	6
2 Chronicles	7	2 John	1	7
2 Chronicles	8	3 John	1	8
2 Chronicles	9	Jude	1	9
2 Chronicles	10	Revelation	1	10
2 Chronicles	11, 12	Revelation	2	11
2 Chronicles	13	Revelation	3	12
2 Chronicles	14, 15	Revelation	4	13
2 Chronicles	16	Revelation	5	14
2 Chronicles	17	Revelation	6	15
2 Chronicles	18	Revelation	7	16
2 Chronicles	19, 20	Revelation	8	17
2 Chronicles	21	Revelation	9	18
2 Chronicles	22, 23	Revelation	10	19
2 Chronicles	24	Revelation	11	20
2 Chronicles	25	Revelation	12	21
2 Chronicles	26	Revelation	13	22
2 Chronicles	27, 28	Revelation	14	23
2 Chronicles	29	Revelation	15	24
2 Chronicles	30	Revelation	16	25
2 Chronicles	31	Revelation	17	26
2 Chronicles	32	Revelation	18	27
2 Chronicles	33	Revelation	19	28
2 Chronicles	34	Revelation	20	29
2 Chronicles	35	Revelation	21	30
2 Chronicles	36	Revelation	22	31

none of his steps shall slide.   SECRET/DECEMBER

DECEMBER	Book	Chapter	Book	Chapter
1	Micah	6	Luke	15
2	Micah	7	Luke	16
3	Nahum	1	Luke	17
4	Nahum	2	Luke	18
5	Nahum	3	Luke	19
6	Habakkuk	1	Luke	20
7	Habakkuk	2	Luke	21
8	Habakkuk	3	Luke	22
9	Zephaniah	1	Luke	23
10	Zephaniah	2	Luke	24
11	Zephaniah	3	John	1
12	Haggai	1	John	2
13	Haggai	2	John	3
14	Zechariah	1	John	4
15	Zechariah	2	John	5
16	Zechariah	3	John	6
17	Zechariah	4	John	7
18	Zechariah	5	John	8
19	Zechariah	6	John	9
20	Zechariah	7	John	10
21	Zechariah	8	John	11
22	Zechariah	9	John	12
23	Zechariah	10	John	13
24	Zechariah	11	John	14
25	Zechariah	12, 13:1	John	15
26	Zechariah	13:2–9	John	16
27	Zechariah	14	John	17
28	Malachi	1	John	18
29	Malachi	2	John	19
30	Malachi	3	John	20
31	Malachi	4	John	21

them that call[a] on the Lord out of a pure heart.

23 But foolish and unlearned questions[c] avoid, knowing that they do gender strifes.

24 And the servant of the Lord must not strive; but be gentle unto all *men*, apt to teach, [β] patient,

25 In meekness[e] instructing those that oppose themselves; if God peradventure[f] will give them repentance to the acknowledging[g] of the truth;

26 And *that* they may [γ]recover themselves out of the snare[i] of the devil, who are taken [δ]captive by him at his will.

CHAPTER III.

THIS know also, that[m] in the last days perilous times shall come.

2 For[e] men shall be lovers of their own selves, covetous, boasters, proud, blasphemers, disobedient to parents, unthankful, unholy,

3 Without natural affection, trucebreakers, [v]false accusers, incontinent, fierce, despisers of those that are good,

4 Traitors,[z] heady, highminded,[u] lovers of pleasures more than lovers of God;

5 Having[w] a form of godliness, but denying the power thereof: from such turn away.

6 For of this sort are they which[v] creep into houses, and lead captive silly women laden with sins, led away with divers lusts,

7 Ever learning, and never able to come to the knowledge of the truth.

8 Now as Jannes and Jambres[a] withstood Moses, so do these also resist the truth: men[b] of corrupt minds, [θ]reprobate concerning the faith.

9 But they shall proceed no further: for their folly shall be manifest unto all men, as their's also was.

10 But thou hast [κ]fully known my doctrine, manner of life, purpose, faith, longsuffering, charity, patience,

11 Persecutions, afflictions, which came unto me at Antioch,[d] at Iconium,[e] at Lystra; what persecutions I endured: but out of *them* all[h] the Lord delivered me.

12 Yea, and all that will live godly in Christ Jesus shall suffer persecution.

13 But evil men and seducers shall wax worse and worse, deceiving, and being[i] deceived.

14 But continue[m] thou in the things which thou hast learned and hast been assured of, knowing of whom thou hast learned *them*;

15 And that from a child thou hast known the holy scriptures, which[o] are able to make thee wise unto salvation through faith which is in Christ Jesus.

16 All[p] scripture *is* given by inspiration of God, and[s] *is* profitable for doctrine, for reproof, for correction, for instruction in righteousness;

17 That the man of God may be perfect,[r] throughly [μ]furnished unto all good works.

CHAPTER IV.

I CHARGE[a] *thee* therefore before God, and the Lord Jesus Christ, who shall

judge[b] the quick and the dead at his appearing and his kingdom;

2 Preach the word; be instant in season, out of season; reprove,[d] rebuke, exhort, with all longsuffering and doctrine.

3 For the time will come when they will not endure sound doctrine; but after their own lusts shall they heap to themselves teachers, having itching ears;

4 And they shall turn away *their* ears from the truth, and shall be turned unto fables.[h]

5 But watch thou in all things,[k] endure afflictions, do the work of an evangelist, [ʃ]make full proof[f] of thy ministry.

6 For I am now ready to be offered, and the time of my departure[m] is at hand.

7 I have fought[p] a good fight, I have finished[q] *my* course, I have kept[r] the faith:

8 Henceforth there is laid up for me a[s] crown[t] of righteousness, which the Lord, the righteous judge, shall give me at that day: and not to me only, but unto all them[w] also that love his appearing.

9 Do thy diligence to come shortly unto me:

10 For Demas hath forsaken me, having loved[z] this present world, and is departed unto Thessalonica; Crescens to Galatia, Titus unto Dalmatia.

11 Only Luke is with me. Take Mark, and bring him with thee; for he is profitable to me for the ministry.

12 And Tychicus[z] have I sent to Ephesus.

13 The cloke that I left at Troas with Carpus, when thou comest bring *with thee*, and the books, *but* especially the parchments.

14 Alexander the coppersmith did me much evil: the Lord[e] reward him according to his works:

15 Of whom be thou ware also; for he hath greatly withstood our [λ]words.

16 At my first answer no man stood with me, but all[ʃ] *men* forsook me: I pray God that it may not be laid[g] to their charge.

17 Notwithstanding the Lord[i] stood with me, and strengthened me; that by me the preaching might be fully known, and *that* all the Gentiles might hear: and I was delivered out of the mouth[k] of the lion.

18 And the Lord[m] shall deliver me from every evil work, and will preserve *me* unto his heavenly kingdom: to whom *be* glory for ever and ever. Amen.

19 Salute Prisca and Aquila, and the household of Onesiphorus.

20 Erastus abode at Corinth: but Trophimus have I left at Miletum sick.

21 Do thy diligence to come before winter. Eubulus greeteth thee, and Pudens, and Linus, and Claudia, and all the brethren.

22 The Lord Jesus Christ *be* with thy spirit. Grace *be* with you. Amen.

The second *epistle* unto Timotheus, ordained the first bishop of the church of the Ephesians, was written from Rome, when Paul was brought before [v]Nero the second time.

Center reference column

A.D. 66.

a 1 Co. 1. 2.
b Re. 20.12,13
c verse 16.
d Tit. 2. 15.
β or, *forbearing*.
e Ga. 6. 1.
f Ac. 8. 22.
g Tit. 1. 1.
γ *awake*.
h 1 Ti. 1. 4.
i 1 Ti. 3. 7.
k chap. 2. 3.
δ *alive*.
ζ or, *fulfil*.
l 1 Ti.4.12,15.
m 1 Ti. 4. 1.
2 Pe. 3. 3.
1 John 2.18.
Jude 17, 18.
n Phi. 1. 23.
2 Pe. 1. 14.
o Ro.1.29..31.
p 1 Ti. 6. 12.
q Ac. 20. 24.
η or, *makebates*.
r Pr. 23. 23.
Re. 3. 10.
s 1 Co. 9. 25.
1 Pe. 5. 4.
Re. 2. 10.
t 2 Pe. 2. 10,
&c.
u Phi. 3. 19.
v 1 Co. 2. 9.
w Tit. 1. 16.
x 1 John 2.15.
y Tit. 1. 11.
z Tit. 3. 12.
a Ex. 7. 11.
b 1 Ti. 6. 5.
θ or, *of no judgment*.
c Ps. 23. 4.
κ or, *been a diligent follower of*.
λ or, *preachings*.
d Ac.13.45,50
e Ac. 14. 5, 6,
19.
f chap. 1.15.
g Ac. 7. 60.
h Ps. 34. 19.
i Mat. 10. 19.
Ac. 23. 11.
k Ps. 22. 21.
l 2 Th. 3. 11.
m Ps. 121. 7.
n chap. 1. 13.
o John 5. 39.
p 2 Pe. 1. 21.
q Ro. 15. 4.
r Ps. 119. 98..
100.
μ or, *perfected*.
a 1 Ti. 5. 21.
6. 13.
v Cæsar Nero,
or, *the Emperor Nero*.

155

Made in the USA
Middletown, DE
08 March 2017